The Anatomy of

yes

To Johnny,

Since Meet,

The Anatomy of

yes

RESORATION OF THE WASTELAND

DESCENT INTO THE UNDERWORLD

DRAGON AND TREASURE

QUEST FOR THE HOLY GRAIL

QUEST FOR IDENTITY

The **Story** Behind Every Sale

Joseph G. Burke

WELLSPRING
North Palm Beach, Florida

wellspring

Published by Wellspring

Design by Madeline Harris

ISBN: 978-1-929266-98-2 (softcover)
ISBN: 978-1-63582-067-6 (ebook)

10   9   8   7   6   5   4   3   2   1

Printed in the United States of America

To Mom, Dad, Ellen, Judith, Jaynie and Jameson.
My once upon a time, and happily ever after.

Contents

FOREWORD

by Thomas S. Monaghan

↓

In 2017, I had a lengthy breakfast with Joseph Burke in downtown Los Angeles. I recall him asking me question after question about how I started Domino's Pizza, the battles we had in growing the company, and about the lessons I had learned. The conversation brought me back to the early days of Domino's, the few dollars I had to start with, the Volkswagen Beetle delivery car, and the delivery niche we filled. When we changed the name from Dominick's to Domino's we had three stores. I actually planned to add a dot on the Domino's logo for each new store we opened. However, given our rapid growth, that plan happily turned out not to be very feasible.

Growing Domino's, owning the Detroit Tigers and starting organizations have genuinely been the work that initially fed my family and also my soul. There have been many hard-fought fights, and I believe this was the story Burke was looking for when we met three years ago. If there was a secret I shared, it was how we instilled consistency in every dimension of Domino's; from the team to the customer to the community.

Burke's book has a lot of insightful questions that every leader at every level should be asking themselves. The answers to these questions are the foundation of your company's story from your first founding days to the legacy it will leave. Whether you are aware of it or not, each day you are writing your own story to your customers, your community, your family and future generations.

This is not light reading. This is for serious Founders, CEOs, and leaders at every level who are courageous enough to read, reflect and look inside themselves to answer the questions posed in the Anatomy of Yes.

Thomas S. Monaghan
Founder of Domino's Pizza

PREFACE

↓

February 28, 2016, 7:44 a.m., Amtrak Station, Fullerton, California

Five months ago I gave a talk to a group of business professionals. A persuasive woman challenged me to write a book on the topic of my talk, archetypal patterns in business. I promised to do so within a year's time. This morning I am boarding a train and heading up and down the coast of California to write that book. I'm traveling alone with an Oakley backpack, an Apple computer, Beats headphones, a Montblanc pen, a detailed outline, and a desire for every organization to discover why they exist. Based on my estimated words per mile, it will take four days on a train to write this book.

I've divided the book into three acts. Act one will explore the five archetypes in the anatomy of yes. Act two will share stories and lessons I learned as a marketing executive at two of *Forbes'* America's 25 Most Inspiring Companies. The third and final act is a call to adventure I hope you accept, as I accepted the same call from a wise and very persuasive person five months ago. This is *The Anatomy of Yes.*

INTRODUCTION

Imagine for a moment you have to persuade a room full of people who are hostile toward your point of view. How would you do it? How would you get them to change their minds?

Our sixteenth president of the United States, Abraham Lincoln, knew how. When he wanted to make a point and get people to agree with him, he didn't start with an argument. Rather, he told them a folksy story that not only changed their minds, but often altered the course of our nation's history. He'd start with the words, "That reminds me of a story," before launching into one of his seemingly endless supply of jokes, anecdotes, and tall tales. From "Somebody call a barber" to the ugliest horseman or someone's prize hog, Lincoln often used the power of stories to explain his policies or win his hearers over to his point of view. Using folksy, down-home wisdom, he got his listeners to laugh—and he got them to say yes.

It's safe to say that most of us would rather hear the word yes to our thoughts, transactions, and points of view. Yet most of us never step back to think about why people give their approval or agreement. Many marketing professionals have attempted to answer this question in a variety of ways, and they have come up with some pretty good answers. But none of them give us a complete picture, which begins with two simple questions:

Why do stories exist?

Why are we magnetized to the beginning, middle, and end of stories?

In sales, customers might say yes to a purchase because of a compelling story, but the reality is, they are doing something more primal. Simply stated, our DNA is hardwired to a recurring three-act story. This story and its distinct archetypal patterns were primally authored to scare us, protect us, and help us find enlightenment.

We might not be aware of it, but we are all currently on our own distinct archetypal hero's journey rife with enemies, allies, and tests. We must accept, understand, and master these archetypal patterns to successfully defeat the "dragons" in business and claim "treasures" in our own professional lives.

In this book we will dissect this story-based hardwiring in our DNA and show how every decision, every yes, is based on a recurring three-act trajectory of *crisis, conflict,* and *resolution.*

You started living this three-act story as an infant, instinctually adjusting the frequencies of your cry to get your mother's attention. You began getting what you wanted in the first thirty minutes after you were born. Your "transactional" life began at birth, and getting what you want in life and in business are fundamentally the same.

In business and sales, a customer's mind approaches every transaction in the same way a hero's mind approaches every battle, every challenge. This base structure is easily lost in an age of big data, in which many companies look at customers as nothing more than a cash-toting herd of tagged animals. Propensity modeling and predictive analytics use statistics and algorithms to monetize people through behavioral triggers. While this type of strategy can be effective in sales, it cannot survive alone, and it is not the root behavior of world-class organizations that embrace every customer as a guest or member of a community. Your customers are on a story-based journey of their own; it's been this way for thousands of years. This book will lead you to discover your own personal powers of persuasion and introduce you to powerful tools you can use to connect your exceptional talents with the incredible quest your customers are on. The root of this knowledge is based in primal thought patterns, not in scripted sales techniques, conditioned responses, semantics, or manipulation.

The revelations, lessons, and questions in this book are based on my own intense quest for yes. The lessons I learned in business started when I was young. Before the age of fourteen I had started three businesses and worked as a paperboy, busboy, and fry cook. I also inherited the good fortune of witnessing the American dream firsthand. My father, an army veteran who could not afford college, launched his career climbing telephone poles in the dead of a Chicago winter, and retired a General Manager at AT&T.

I have read many business books that left me walking away saying, "Interesting, but so what?" This is not that book. There are questions titled "Your Quest for Yes" at the end of each chapter written for you to find your own anatomy of yes. Answer each of these questions, either with pen and paper or at anatomyofyes.com/story. Do not spend too much time pondering each answer; we are looking for your instinctive response. When you are done, gather with other leaders in your organization who have done the same and review a chapter each week. By doing so, you will statistically increase the odds of serving more—and selling more.

Act I

The Five Archetypes in the Anatomy of Yes

1

Why Does a Parent Die in the First 15 Minutes of Disney Movies?

↓

Disney movies, full of animation, imagination, and memorable music, are universally loved and quickly become classics. But have you ever wondered why a parent dies in a Disney movie, often within the first fifteen minutes? Think about it: *Finding Nemo*, *Bambi*, and *The Lion King* all include a brutal scene in which a parent is taken from a child. Why? Why are Hiro Hamada's parents dead in the Disney-Pixar movie *Big Hero 6*, and then his brother is killed in the first act? More important, how does this translate into a powerful yes that drives people to this multibillion-dollar entertainment empire known as Disney, which has fueled so many movies, TV shows, parks, and merchandise for more than sixty years?

Disney movies follow and attract their audiences with the same time-tested structure of every campfire story, movie, book, and myth. It's why they work. Stories begin with a person living their life as they know it, when something dramatic and life-changing happens. This person, or protagonist, is called into an adventure to face enemies, allies, and tests. Each of these tests also follows the same arc of crisis, conflict, and resolution. The structure of story is simple; the content of story, because humans are involved, is complex.

So, what does this have to do with business? How can this understanding help you with your customers? Before we can answer this question, let's first peel back the layers and learn why stories and storytelling exist.

After the blockbuster success of Disney's first fully animated film, *Snow White and the Seven Dwarfs*, Walt and his brother Roy built a house for their parents. Shortly after moving in, Walt's mother complained about fumes from the gas furnace. Repairmen were called, but the problem wasn't properly addressed. A few days later Walt and Roy's parents were hospitalized, and their mother, Flora, died as a result of asphyxiation from the fumes. Walt and Roy felt a deep sense of grief over losing their mother, a grief that stayed with them for the rest of their lives. Could Flora Disney be the reason Walt Disney's storylines are rooted in the death of a parent? Was this Walt's way of dealing with the tragedy?

Disney's fourth animated feature, *Dumbo*, is another great example. Dumbo, the young circus elephant, is ridiculed for his big ears. His mother, Mrs. Jumbo attempts to protect him, but her actions cause the Ringmaster to lock her up and separates him from his mother. Voilà, the story fits.

What about *The Little Mermaid*? Ariel has no mother. She follows a quest to leave her father and her life under the sea and walk like a human. In *Bambi*, the mother is shot dead, leaving Bambi alone and full of grief. And yet Bambi pushes through this grief to find a deeper meaning to his life and eventually become lord of the forest. In *Finding Nemo* the mother dies in the first ten minutes.

Stories without parents have been—and will be—around for a long time. Disney has the ability to retell an old story with beautiful animation and songs. But there are many, many more. Mark Twain's Tom Sawyer and Huck Finn novels, C. S. Lewis' Narnia tales, and J. K. Rowling's Harry Potter series all feature at least one missing parent.

All this begs the question: Do truly original stories exist, or are they all retellings of ancient tales?

Even William Shakespeare's comedies, romances, and histories all were retellings of ancient stories. Shakespeare is best known for his play *Romeo and Juliet*, but it was actually a remake of a story that originated in the fifteenth century. *The Tempest*, which was one of his last plays, had an original plot, but he also drew inspiration from the literature of his day.

THE PLOT THICKENS

In order to understand why stories are so powerful, we must talk about Carl Jung's "collective unconscious" and how it relates to arriving at a yes in business and in life.

According to Jung, the collective unconscious is our innate table of contents, so to speak. He believed that we are all born into this world with an unconscious understanding of stories critical to our survival, one of which is what Joseph Campbell calls the hero's journey. The hero, or protagonist, goes on a journey from a narrow point of view to a wider point of view or knowledge. Celtic culture calls this the immram, or "soul journey." Heroes in stories all go through these soul journeys—they are faced with enemies, allies, and tests. You are likely in the middle of one right now.

The hero takes on an ordeal. He succeeds at certain tests, fails at others. When he finally overcomes the ordeal, he possesses new knowledge and a new wisdom. We are all currently on this same soul journey, an adventure or ordeal with tests, enemies, and allies. We listen to, watch, and tag along with heroes in stories because their adventure echoes our own. We know when we have completely overcome an ordeal; it is that moment when we share the lesson and tell the story to another person going through a similar ordeal. That's why stories without parents or with parents dying are so common—they recall ancient archetypal patterns.

ONCE UPON A TIME . . .

Archetypes' roots can be traced back to the Greek philosopher Plato and run through the modern works of Jung's collective unconscious. The word *archetype* is de-rived from the Greek ἀρχέτυπος (archétupos), meaning "original form" or "first molded." Archetypal patterns can be found in every story ever told, whether handed down orally, written, or filmed, in which a hero, or protagonist, goes on a daring journey or quest. Along the way the hero must overcome fear and reach enlightenment. Neurologically, fMRI scans show that both fear and enlightenment compete for the same space in the brain.[1] Fear releases a hormone called cortisol, while enlightenment, or gratitude, releases the neurotransmitters serotonin and dopamine.

The fear in these tales comes from moments of crisis that drive the hero to greater things:

A parent dies; a bank is robbed; a child is kidnapped.

We are immediately glued to these stories because any of these

---

[1] Alex Korb, PhD, *The Upward Spiral: Using Neuroscience to Reverse the Course of Depression, One Small Change at a Time* (Oakland, Calif.: New Harbinger Publications, 2015).

fearful things could happen to us. Stories take us on a journey or arc of crisis, conflict, and resolution; this is where we find enlightenment and how we overcome fear.

To back up this point, psychiatrists Thomas Holmes and Richard Rahe researched the validity of stress as a predictor of illness. They tested different populations within the United States with African, Mexican, and Native American groups. The scale was also tested cross-culturally, comparing Japanese and Malaysian groups with American populations. Through their research, they developed the Social Readjustment Rating Scale, also called the Holmes and Rahe Stress Scale.[2]

As you might guess, the death of a spouse ranks number one on the stress scale, inducing 100 life stress units. This is followed by divorce at 73 and marital separation at 65. To give a sense of scale, imprisonment will inflict 63 life stress units, death of a close family member 63, retirement 45 stress units, pregnancy 40, trouble with a boss 32, trouble in with in-laws 29, and even a speeding ticket will yield 11 life stress units. Are you beginning to recognize some of the storylines of movies, books, and TV shows?

Applying this practically, I recently developed a strategy for a mortgage lending company by using the example of a customer who was buying a home (32 life stress units) due to a job change (39 life stress units), which required a move (20 life stress units), who then found out they were having a child (39 life stress units). Bam, there's 130 life stress units, just 20 units away from 150. Experiencing at least 150 life stress units in a one-year period

---

[2] *Wikipedia*, s.v. "Holmes and Rahe Stress Scale," last modified January 11, 2018, https://en.wikipedia.org/wiki/Holmes_and_Rahe_stress_scale.

will give you a 50 percent chance of developing an illness, while 300 or more units in a year will give you a 90 percent chance of developing a stress-related illness or mental breakdown.

For young people, the story is a little different. Knowing what we now know about parents dying in Disney movies, it's no surprise that the number one stressor on the Holmes and Rahe scale for children/non-adults is the death of a parent, which is tied with an unplanned pregnancy or abortion at 100 life stress units.

What captivates children about Disney movies and time-tested stories such as *Finding Nemo* and *The Little Mermaid* is the young hero's crisis of losing a parent and the opportunity to venture out on their own. Parents unwittingly share stories with their children so they will know how to survive without them. For example, in the movie *Home Alone*, Macaulay Culkin's young character is left home alone without his parents to take on a series of "tests" by two thieves, or "enemies."

How does all this apply to business? Keep reading—the next chapter will begin to answer that question.

2

The Business of Storyteling

↓

Each of your customers is on their own hero's journey, on a quest for something greater. Every customer is on a quest to overcome a barrier, conquer a fear, or reach a state of enlightenment. They want to say yes to a product or service that will feed that narrative, even if it's purchasing something as mundane as a hammer, a pair of shoes, or paper towels.

Remember, in business, it is your organization's role to empower the hero (your customer) with a "sharper sword" to defeat a dangerous "dragon." Sound a little heady or esoteric? Let's look at a simple example such as Bounty paper towels. I remember hearing the ad as a kid: "Bounty, the quicker picker-upper." Clever. The customer, as the hero, has a crisis: a mess. What does the hero need? A paper towel that quickly overcomes the problem and cleans up the mess. If you remember the TV spots, the competitor's paper towel was compared with the far superior Bounty paper towel. The competitor's paper towel would fill up with liquid and fall apart into a pulpy mess. This posed a conflict for the hero. The Bounty paper towel, with great celerity, sweeps up the puddled mess with just one swipe. A victory over the ordeal—conflict solved. Sounds silly, but this well-constructed anatomy of yes made the customer the hero and the product an empowering weapon to "restore a waste-land." These instinctual story arcs are hardwired into our brains—our collective unconscious. (By the way, after twenty years, Bounty brought back the campaign "Bounty, the quicker picker-upper.")

Have you ever heard the phrase "I've fallen, and I can't get up"? If so, you've seen the late-night TV commercial featuring elderly people wearing an alarm that allows them to alert the paramedics when they fall and injure themselves. It's the stuff memes are made of, but underlying it is a key hero-empowerment story. The hero is actually the adult child of the elderly person, the crisis is the necessity of the elderly person living alone, and the con-flict is the guilt the adult child feels for not being there. The precaution of this alert device releases the guilt, bringing resolution and restoring the son or daughter's role of hero, protecting their parent from harm. This campaign has been so effective, it has run for almost thirty years.

Let's get up-to-date and look at some Super Bowl ads. One recurring theme in these ads is using babies comedically to sell products. Why do we pay attention to babies? Why do we all watch the movements of a young child dressed up like Darth Vader in the famous Volkswagen ad? Because the human brain's primary visual cortex, or V1, is wired to recognize and process the image of a child's face milliseconds before anything else. E-Trade, Evian, Doritos, and the NFL all ran Super Bowl ads featuring babies. We are wired this way to protect our species, our genome, our future generations, and our legacy. We also protect the species by passing on cautionary and inspiring lessons in the form of stories. The brands Kia (featuring Pierce Brosnan), Bud Light (the Bud Knight), and Tide (David Harbour and Terry Bradshaw) all aired Super Bowl ads that deconstructed the elements of story; whether they realized it or not, they were playing our consciousness like a needle bouncing on a vinyl record of a familiar song.

THE POWER OF STORY IN BUSINESS

Now that we understand the power of story in the lives of human beings, let's connect the dots to how we go about applying the power of stories in business.

We can begin by asking a few simple questions: What story is our company telling? How do we tell it? Do potential customers and clients understand it? Can they integrate that story with their own?

Let's begin with the first part of the story: the crisis point. What pain in the marketplace does your company address? Who are your competitors, and what products and services cause conflict for someone trying to make a buying decision? (Don't say you have no competition—you do.) What solution (resolution) or repeatable promise does your company deliver? The fewer words you can use to answer this, the better.

1. **Crisis** (pain in the market based on the highest life stress units):

2. **Conflict** (competitors who offer similar products and services):

3. **Resolution** (repeatable promise or solution your organization delivers):

Once you nail down what these are, you will have the three basic plot points of your organization's story. Think of it as your archetypal org chart. Would every person in your organization answer these three questions the same? If not, this is a sign of an organization that has not yet discovered or clearly communicated the reason they exist.

THE FIVE ARCHETYPES IN THE ANATOMY OF YES

There are five archetypal patterns that form a living storyline between you and your customers. You may not be aware of this storyline, but it began the day your organization was conceived of and founded. These five archetypal patterns form the construct of every story ever told, and they occur every day in business and in life.

1. The Quest for Identity
2. The Dragon and Treasure
3. The Descent into the Underworld
4. The Restoration of the Wasteland
5. The Quest for the Holy Grail

Before we look at the storyline and archetype of your organization, let's gain an understanding of how transactions occur.

THE DECISION CYCLE

Everything a customer has ever purchased follows the same purchase decision cycle. The cycle starts with *awareness*, when the customer becomes aware the product or service exists. The second step is *consideration*, when the customer considers whether to purchase the product or service. The third is *shopping*, when the customer compares, researches, and shops for the product or service. The fourth is the act of *buying*, when the customer purchases the product or service. And the fifth and final step is *loving*, when the customer either loves, hates, or is indifferent about their purchase. What makes this cycle effective is proper execution. If the customer loves the product or service they purchased, they will use it and tell other people about it; this is the most powerful form of awareness. In this cycle, loving feeds awareness.

The next step is to plot every touch point a customer experiences throughout the decision cycle, which allows you to track the emotional journey of the customer. What you end up building are true customer experiences that have nothing to do with the actual product. That may sound counterproductive, but consider Amazon's model. Outside of its media offerings, Amazon doesn't make anything. It delivers products through a self-described "customer-obsessed" experience and guarantees the highest level of satisfaction. Every organization is capable of delivering the same elevated customer experience Amazon does, but they often let their products get in the way.

Archetypal patterns exist in every product, transaction, and personal relationship you have. In the following chapters, we will explore each pattern in detail and why it matters to you, your organization, and most important, your customers. This knowledge is based on the patterns our minds have operated on for many thousands of years; they are not strategies developed for manipulating people into a onetime sale. Companies that rely solely on data to provide clues about the buying habits of consumers might give customers what they want, but they won't empower them with what they need.

As you read through the five archetypes, see if you can connect your organization's own story with each one. When you understand the archetypal reason your organization exists, you will better understand how to serve your customers and propel their own hero's journey. The five archetypes are why your company makes products and services, and why it generates revenue.

The more you interact with this book, the more you will learn about your organization, and the more you will learn about yourself. Consider this a call to adventure.

3

The Quest for Identity

↓

The first archetype in the anatomy of yes is the Quest for Identity. In stories, a hero feels out of place, is reluctant to take on a challenge, or senses that there is a missing piece of their identity that leads to great meaning. This archetype has been played out in popular books and movies such as *The Matrix, The Bourne Identity*, and *Alice in Wonderland*. The hero's journey takes the hero from a narrow understanding of themselves to a greater understanding.

Your company's quest for identity started the moment it became an entity, just as your personal quest for identity began the moment you were born. In the early stages of your company you defined a purpose, a reason the business existed. Your company provides someone with something in a unique and identifiable way. To identify the way in which your organization transacts, you gave it a name. Your company's identity might be the name of an original founder, a product, a nonsensical word, or a word that has changed identity with the growth of a company or new markets it enters.

George Eastman named his camera and film company Kodak, a word that has no significance but is unique and identifiable.

GEICO got its name from Government Employees Insurance Company. The internet streaming company Skype formed its name and identity through the technical term "sky peer-to-peer," which evolved from Skyper. The list goes on and on, but the same pattern emerges: A name was given to the entity to form its identity.

In the battle for identity, many companies create a name that will be memorable and invoke meaning. One example is the telecommunications company Verizon, which forms its identity through the Latin root word *veritas* (truth) and the word *horizon*. For organizations such as law firms, the name evolves, get shortened, or changes when a partner leaves. The quest for identity is so powerful, the ride-share company Lyft delayed its launch until it could legally own the word *Lyft*.

In the early days, as your company struggled to find its identity, a mark or logo became associated with the business. This mark, or branding, became a symbol that identifies the company in a simple but very powerful way. Think of the symbol of an apple with a bite taken out of it. Brand identities and logos are the most powerful symbols that magnetize the human mind to reliable and consistent physiological experiences. In literature, a symbol is described as a concrete representation of a sensory experience that goes on to suggest a further meaning. Your organization's symbol, or logo, is no different. It represents a sensory experience and a reputation for delivering it. For example, if you travel from country to country and see a Starbucks symbol, you immediately are transported to a consistent sensory experience—a specific smell, taste, and awakening elicited by that symbol.

The power of your organization's symbol in the Quest for Identity archetype will lead customers to view your products, services, and brand as ways to inspire, construct, and define their own personal identity. That's why it's so important to look at the genesis of your company and be able to clearly define why it exists.

Consumer, apparel, and fashion brands are examples of companies that always empower the customer's journey in their quest for identity.

When I was the national brand director for Disney Store, it became obvious that we were not selling shirts, pajamas, and toys—we were selling an identity based on a child's imagination in becoming a princess or a pirate. Owning a *High School Musical* T-shirt wasn't about buying a T-shirt, it was about being part of a movement and community that danced in unison, harmonizing the ideal: "We're all in this together."

GENERATION MARKS

In 2000, as an equity partner in a dotcom start-up called Joe Explorer, I played the role of Joe Explorer in a Travel Channel–like show. The concept was to explore the world in search of adventure and sell adventure travel packages. The audience would follow my archetypal character, Joe Explorer, as he sojourned into the unknown, and they would become inspired to seek out their own journey.

We traveled to French Polynesia and danced with the native Tahitians, biked to the top of Mount Rotui, and swam with live sharks. While on a massive catamaran in Cook's Bay with a native Tahitian named Henri, I asked about the significance of his tattoos. He explained that they are "generation marks." Henri told me that tattoos on Tahiti were traditionally made by hollowing out a shark's tooth, tapping the tooth into the skin, and pouring a burning hot plant dye into the skin. This was a rite of passage for young warriors. The markings each generation had tattooed on their skin were specific to their generation—their identity.

Today we see a similar trend. In 2016 America, Pew Research tells us that 36 percent of millennials have tattoos, as opposed to 21 percent of Gen X (those born in the 1960s and 1970s) who have tattoos, body piercings other than their ears, or untraditional hair dye. The millennial generation is the largest in US history, and they are far more likely to seek out markings that define their identity. Knowing this, the smartest companies engage their customers in communities and movements with very specific identities that live within the "skin" of the brand; think of Harley-Davidson (leather riding vests), Lululemon (yoga pants), and Vans (checker-pattern shoes).

YOUR QUEST FOR YES

1. Is there a story behind your company's mark or logo?
2. What were the early struggles that defined your company's identity?
3. What does your company have a reputation for doing better and more consistently than anyone else?

4

The Dragon and Treasure

↓

The second archetype, the Dragon and Treasure, occurs when the hero must overcome or defeat the dragon to capture a treasure. Of the five archetypes in the anatomy of yes, this is the most common, and it's a recurring theme in all action-adventure stories and films; and also the most common archetype in business. The "dragon" manifests in many forms—it might be a menacing beast, an enemy, a tyrannical king, a ghost, or a personal dragon such as addiction or a negative self-concept. As the story goes, the hero must use weapons, skills, and wisdom to defeat these dragons.

As a business or brand, you want to position your products or services in such a way that your customers understand that you are offering them a "sharper sword," capable of defeating these dangerous dragons. The best brands do this—look at Nike's Just Do It and Find Your Greatness. Or think of Gatorade's Fuel to Power Your Game. These companies empower the customer (hero) with the battle gear, weapons, and tools necessary to defeat the competitor (dragon). I recently saw a spot for GoPro cameras; their tagline is Be a Hero. Even though their stock took a hit in 2016, they get it.

I had a recent conversation with an executive at Toastmasters International. They have almost sixteen thousand chapters in 142 countries. They are doing exceptional work helping two distinct groups of people: those working in corporate jobs looking to advance their careers, and those looking for personal development. We landed on the fact that corporate Toastmasters members are looking to empower their communication skills to defeat dragons and discover a treasure through job advancement and a higher salary. We also concluded that Toastmasters members looking for personal achievement were on a quest for identity as they sought to find their true self and better communicate that to others.

The many stories and movies that center on the Dragon and Treasure archetype dig deep into the heart of the hero. Organizations need to look at the customer as the hero, and specifically identify the customer's fears, address them, and understand the customer's archetypal need for the company's product or service.

If you are thinking your business is not entrenched in this archetype, keep exploring. Here are some examples:

A bicycle company (Trek, Specialized, Santa Cruz Bicycles). If a customer demands a high level of performance for competition or personal bests, the bicycle is no different from Luke Skywalker's X-wing fighter. Just like the X-wing fighter, a performance bicycle allows the rider to surmount obstacles against competitors who strive to achieve the same treasure, or a gold medal on the podium. The smartphone tracking app STRAVA awards virtual gold medals for riders' who compete against each other; another form of treasure. Incidentally, I know some riders who swear by their old-school mountain bikes; they are no different than Han Solo and his pride for the *Millennium Falcon*.

Medical device companies (Medtronic, Danaher, Edwards Lifesciences). Oncologists wield medical devices with the same precision and skill as Bradley Cooper did portraying the true-life hero Chris Kyle in the film *American Sniper*. Physicians, like great swordsmen, become masterful in using their hands and medical devices to defeat dragons such as cancer, coronary disease, and heart failure.

Consumer electronics companies (Microsoft, Samsung, and Vizio). Laptops, smartphones, and smart TVs—these are the modern-day weapons and communication outposts of business. In 490 BC, sending a message with the subject line "We beat the Persians" required a 26.2-mile run from Marathon to Athens, Greece.

Think about the last time you held your breath and hit the send button on an email, knowing the information was a potential cannonball to the organization, or the last time you received an email confirming the close of a deal you'd worked on for two years. These critical emails are delivered no differently than the messages of sprinters from Marathon—they just get there a whole lot faster.

BATTLE OF THE BRANDS

Look closely at how Nike positions its shoes in the minds of athletes. When Nike says "Find Your Greatness" in a pair of shoes, it is no different from an ancient story in which the wise master sword maker hands a young warrior a shiny sword and says, "Find your greatness," as he sends the warrior into battle.

Imagine the same master sword maker saying, "Just do it"—the same impact is delivered. This is the most common archetype in business, and the storyline with which brands do the most battle.

One of the most talked-about ads in history is the famous Apple commercial from 1984. The ad's root archetype was a literal expression of free thought slaying the dragon of Orwellian conformity with a sledgehammer. Steve Jobs instinctually understood archetypal patterns in everything he designed—he never sold gadgets or devices; instead he sold "ease of use" for artists and warriors alike to create greatness, overcome barriers, and defeat dragons. In my case, Jobs consistently armed me with the weapons, paintbrushes, and canvases to do what I do best. These weapons were my first Macintosh computer, iPod, and iPhone; they have been the most powerful tools in bringing my ideas, writings, and ad campaigns to life. And yes, I do see Steve Jobs as the master who used media events to theatrically reveal each shiny new sword to his customers as they went into battle. If you are a loyal Apple customer, he handed you these swords and said, "Think different."

The Dragon and Treasure archetype is powerful, because all organizations are based on the battlefield of sales. Without sales, your company does not exist. When we create "archetypal journey maps" for organizations, we dig deep into the storylines of this archetype; this is the story every sales force needs to be aligned with and live by. This is a simple illustration of an organization's archetypal journey map, it meticulously follows the customers' journey from awareness of a product to purchase and loving. It also follows the structure of every three act story.

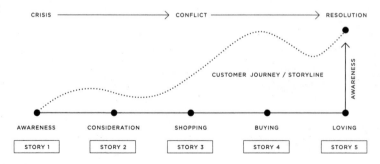

ARCHETYPAL JOURNEY MAP

YOUR QUEST FOR YES

1. What journeys are your customers on that require weapons?

2. What weapons does your organization equip customers with?

3. What companies have supplied you with weapons and tools you personally use every day to overcome barriers and slay the dragons in your life?

5

The Descent into the Underworld

↓

The third archetype, Descent into the Underworld, can be both figurative and literal. The descent is the hero's lowest point on their quest; a point where they doubt themselves, face internal and external demons, or experience their deepest despair. You'll know it when you experience it for yourself. Recall the Holmes and Rahe Stress Scale—these are descents into the depths of the underworld that pound at your soul and test your will. A death of a family member, an illness, financial ruin, and being terminated or laid off are all examples.

In literature, heroes always experience one or more descents into the underworld. This occurs in classical literature such as Homer's "The Odyssey," when Odysseus descends into Hades, and in modern storytelling such as the popular series "Stranger Things," where children discover the "Upside Down"–a menacing parallel dimension they can access by descending into caves beneath them.

Disney's *Inside Out* takes us inside and personifies the mental states of eleven-year-old Riley as she deals with a traumatic move and the fracturing of the parent-child relationship. While a parent is not killed in this film, the story was influenced by writer

and director Pete Docter's own traumatic move to Denmark as a
child. Docter had his own personal descent into the underworld
in the development of the film as well. He had great characters
for the story, yet he struggled to identify how the movie would
end. He wrestled with what statement the film was making.
Nothing seemed to be working, and he reached a point where
he felt like he would either quit or be fired. He took a long walk
in the woods, considering what would happen if either of those
scenarios came to be. And as he thought about the ramifications
in his own life and the range of emotions he would experience,
he suddenly saw how they fit with the message of the film. That
walk gave him the ending for the film he had been searching for,
and it also clarified the film's message. He ascended, and so goes
the story.

In consumer products, this archetype plays directly into alcohol and other mind-altering products. Have a look at liquor
ads—they are often fantasy experiences with dark and cryptic
imagery. A descent into the underworld takes the customer-hero
out of their everyday life and transforms them into an alternative
state of consciousness. Watch television spots from Kraken rum;
they have an eerie computer-animated octopus. Bacardi shows
dark, almost vampire-like print ads with the Bacardi bottle juxta-
posed with dragons, guns and atom bombs, and the scotch whis-
ky brand Johnnie Walker is one of the world's best-selling spirits
by a long shot, bringing in over $4 billion in annual sales. Here's
how the Johnnie Walker story starts on their own website:

The year was 1819 and John Walker's father had just died. A
tough start for a humble farm lad, you might think, but there

was always something special about John. A glint in his eye, a fire
in his belly, a spring in step perhaps.

The Johnnie Walker story is told by actor Robert Carlyle. Notice how the arc of the story starts with crisis and fear as Johnnie
Walker's father dies, then, with "a glint in his eye," he journeys
for enlightenment. The powerful brand story of Johnnie Walker
follows the recurring pattern of crisis, conflict, and resolution in
fewer than fifty words.

There are also two sides to this for companies. Alcohol brands
can drive customers deeper into the "underworld" of alcoholism
and addiction. Organizations such as Promises and Alcoholics
Anonymous have an express purpose to recuse those who have
fallen into the depths of addiction, or the underworld.

From my own experiences in the underworld of epic fails, I
brought back the ability to simplify the space between steps in a
process. I was lucky to share this ability with a number of college
students. For four years, I worked with Professor John Jackson
at California State University, Fullerton, who runs an incubator
and a student consulting program that builds a business plan for
companies over the course of a semester. When I mentored these
amazing young university students, the first order of business
was to begin building their semester-ending project and presentation on the first day. Many of these students are the first members of their family to attend college, and their hunger to succeed,
work, and learn is infectious.

On the first day of the semester, we played a question-and-
answer game in which everyone took an imaginary walk in the
woods and encountered enemies, allies, and tests. Based on the

answers, the team would designate a leader and a "keeper of the story," someone to build the PowerPoint presentation to be given at the end of the semester. We then cast each student as a character in the storyline and would direct their research to fulfilling a "chapter" in the story. This was glorious work that improved with each semester. At one final presentation that these students gave to a company, a CEO was schooled by a team of wide-eyed students in front of his board members. One of the key learnings they shared with the CEO was a plan to reawaken more than one hundred of their best customers who had not been contacted in over two years. It was one of the most fulfilling stories to watch unfold as these bright young students opened this CEO's eyes to a fallow wasteland that was ripe with sales opportunities (treasures), ready to reap. They served that organization well and empowered the CEO. The experience also showed me that if you want to be an expert in something, you need to mentor someone.

Through this experience, I learned that when you are looking for people to hire, it's best to find people with passion and integrity—the only two things you cannot teach. If a person has these two things, they can learn anything.

To sharply focus on the Descent into the Underworld archetype, products either enable a customer's descent into the underworld or enable customers to rise from it. Working with a mortgage lender, we discovered that the most powerful customer retention tool was delivering unexpected value to the customer in what we called the Valley of Uncertainty. This was a carbon copy of the Descent into the Underworld archetype, as we mapped the emotional state of home buyers.

Through exhaustive journey mapping, we traced the customer-hero's journey from the moment of the loan prequalification letter to the move-in date of a home buyer. We discovered a massive gap between "awareness" and "buying" where the loan officers lost valuable contact with the loan prospects. We realized that it was vital to intimately identify and address the top local real estate brokerage servicing most of the home loan prospects. We called this stage "early intervention"—forging a successful relationship by romancing top local Realtors® who had loan prospects sitting shotgun with them on their quest to find a home. The next stage of the process was what we called "crossing the threshold"; here the emotional state of the buyer increases in both excitement (adrenaline) and anxiety (cortisol). We scored the emotion of fear in new home buyers as they crossed this archetypal threshold, using a scale that ranged from a fear of losing the loan, to not finding a home, to getting beat by cash buyers, to ultimately experiencing buyer's remorse after closing on a home. We saw again how the Realtor had great influence on these fears, either allaying or amplifying them.

The next stage stood as a gateway to the Valley of Uncertainty. This is the period when fears are at the highest level. We also identified this as the best opportunity for the bank to build a relationship with the home buyer, because discouraged buyers are looking for validation, inspiration, and some much-needed comic relief. The methodology here had to be precise—not just communicating these virtues to the prospective buyer, but authentically driving value from the bank to the Realtor when the buyer's positive emotions were at an all-time low. This systematic, authentic strategy of service resulted in a 67 percent increase in business between the two organizations (mortgage brokers and Realtors) in less than six months.

Watching, listening, and reacting to your customer's descent into the underworld exposes the greatest opportunity to truly serve more and sell more.

YOUR QUEST FOR YES

1. What do your customers fear most?
2. How does your product or service protect them from this fear?

6

Restoration of the Wasteland

↓

The fourth archetype in the anatomy of yes is the Restoration of the Wasteland. It occurs when the hero comes upon a place or situation that is in unrest. The hero struggles but eventually restores the wasteland to its original state. This archetype is played out in films such as *Gladiator*, *The Road Warrior*, and every installment of *Alien*, in which the hero comes upon a planet overwrought with parasitic monsters and then nukes from orbit.

The restoration of the wasteland exists in business as products and services that fix problems, restore things to their former glory, or simply clean up a mess. Good examples of the Restoration of the Wasteland archetype are online services such as Priceline and VRBO. Both these brands take unprofitable space such as hotel rooms and vacation rentals and restore them to profitability. Priceline, to this day, uses William Shatner as the Negotiator. This is a perfect use of a business archetype—the Negotiator fights for the buyer and the seller to restore otherwise wasted space.

This archetype is also prominent in the mental health, counseling and legal space. Attorneys often take on the role of a hero fighting and defending a person, property, or place that has been hit with ruin.

Businesses, products, and brands can take on more than one archetype, but there is always a primary archetype. In our work at Goodwill Industries, we trademarked a campaign I wrote called "Find the Good." This harmonized two restorations; people and things. For the material (clothing) donor, the archetype was Restoration of the Wasteland, in that Goodwill takes people's old stuff and turns it into work and revenues to support and employ people with physical and cognitive disabilities. It was also key message to the Goodwill store shopper: "You will 'Find the Good' if you shop our stores; you will find rare and hidden treasures where you least expect them." And it's true—there are many stories of people finding valuable works of art at Goodwill. For instance, a Massachusetts man bought a three-dollar painting at his local Goodwill that went for $194,000 at auction.

Goodwill Industries itself was founded on the Restoration of the Wasteland archetype through elevating people. In 1902, Edgar Helms sat in an alley in Boston and witnessed old furniture and goods being thrown into alleys, and during the Great Depression, Helms also saw people with disabilities left jobless and broke, figuratively thrown into an alley. Helms created the most powerful social enterprise by restoring people and things that others saw as waste.

Human beings are not innately wired to restore wastelands. Rather, it is a function of ethical or spiritual inspiration met with great skill in battling dragons. Companies who authentically engage in corporate social responsibility programs, philanthropic investments, and direct social enterprise are really heroes themselves using their captured treasures to engage in a restoration of the wasteland. Similar to Goodwill Industries, the company

Toms shoes promises, "With every product you purchase, Toms will help a person in need. One for One."

Although Toms has added causes to its root messaging, its mantra and story remains consistent: One for One®. This is also a modern and millennial restoration of the wasteland, and the delta of millennial desires intersecting with millennial values: Look cool and save the world. Toms continues to consistently tell this story well as it works around the world in a restoration of the wasteland and endows each customer in their own quest for identity by continually updating its shoe designs and styles.

On the other, slightly darker side, marketers and advertisers often use this archetype as a crude crowbar for commerce. Every "before and after" advertisement, every fear-based commercial warning customers of imminent doom, and every infomercial plays and preys upon restoring a wasteland, exposing a situation such as dirty shower tiles as a bigger danger than it really is. Just watch a latenight infomercial and you will see this archetype played out repeatedly, often with great success. The infomercial will start with overdramatizing the crisis, saying something like, "Tired of dirty shower tiles that store infectious mold and mildew?" Next you'll see the conventional conflict of scrubbing tile the old-fashioned way, and finally, with one spray of the product, the mold is gone! This is a simplistic and almost juvenile restoration, but it's powerful because it follows an archetypal pattern.

For world-class organizations, a restoration of the wasteland story is best told through exposing the unseen value in the wasteland itself. The organizations that accomplish this most effectively are charitable, such as Homes for Our Troops, Big Brothers Big Sisters of America, and Boys & Girls Clubs of America. These organizations see the opportunity in forgotten people, and seek to restore what is intrinsically good in them.

Your company does not need to be a nonprofit to tell this story. Restoring the wasteland may be a second or third chapter in your company's story of yes.

YOUR QUEST FOR YES

1. In what ways is your organization in the business of restoring something?
2. How do your products and services fix problems, restore things to their former glory, or clean up messes for your customers and clients?
3. What products, services, or professionals have helped rescue you from your own personal wasteland?

7

The Quest for the Holy Grail

↓

The fifth and final archetype in the anatomy of yes is the Quest for the Holy Grail; this is the hero's quest for eternal life. We have seen this cinematically played out in Steven Spielberg's *Indiana Jones* and the *Last Crusade,* in which Harrison Ford's character overcomes a maze of tests, enemies, and allies to recover the holy grail, believed to possess eternal life.

The earliest recording of a Holy Grail archetype dates back to the twelfth-century story of Percival. In the poem, the holy grail is used to heal the Fisher King, whom he encounters on a journey home to see his mother. Although it is commonly thought that Jesus Christ used the grail in the Last Supper, this story is not supported by any accounts in ancient or modern-day versions of the Bible, nor does the Catholic Church give any credence to the legend. We do see the archetype of the ancient grail appear as the Philosopher's Stone in Harry Potter, and poet T. S. Eliot cites the story of Percival and the healing of the Fisher King as a symbolic canvas in his poem *The Waste Land.*

The Holy Grail archetype appears all over literature, stories, brands, and products and within every person's own archetypal journey. The quest for eternal life is as old as recorded history itself and manifests in thousands of modern forms—from the Heaven's Gate cult in San Diego killing themselves with phenobarbital and vodka while wearing matching Nike shoes to scientific forms of eternal life, including biotech and cryogenic freezing. *Holy grail* is also an often-used term for something that possesses secret powers or a mythical solution to an impossible problem.

THE BUSINESS OF HOLY GRAILS

In business, holy grail brands and products are health, wellness, and antiaging products and procedures, and any products or services to be used posthumously to tell the story or legacy of a person. Your customer, as the hero, is on a quest for a product, service, or knowledge that will make them healthier, live longer, and leave a legacy based on their hero's journey. The Quest for the Holy Grail may not be your company's primary archetype, but there are holy grails embedded in every organization.

Young people do not seek holy grails, nor do youth brands. Youth brands are based on exuberance, virility, a magnetic sense of attraction, and a mantra of YOLO (you only live once). The Quest for the Holy Grail archetype is the story told to "kings" who seek to extend their reign as "ruler of the land." Literally, this story has been told to lead customers in search of products that hold the power to make them look younger, live longer, and leave a lasting legacy on earth.

In the quest to look younger, Americans spend more than $8 billion annually on cosmetic surgery procedures. The top procedure among women is breast augmentation. Although women may find this procedure improves physical attractiveness, something deeper is at play: A larger breast size is a biological sign of fertility. In a recent *Psychology Today* article, Vinita Mehta, PhD, explains that "indeed, there is a positive association between levels of estradiol, a fertility-related hormone, and larger breast size; in turn, the combination of larger breasts and a smaller waist-to-hip ratio seems to be linked to a significantly greater likelihood of conceiving."[3] At its root, cosmetic surgery is the customer's quest to look more fertile, youthful, and better equipped to bear life.

In the quest to leave a legacy on earth, there are companies that create financial plans and trusts for families in the event of death, charitable organizations that market a bequest from financial donors in exchange for their name on a building, and even some new players in the legacy space that cryogenically freeze a person's brain in the event it can be unfrozen in the future. These companies all create products and services promising the fountain of youth and the prospect of living beyond a human's natural life on earth.

YOUR QUEST FOR YES

1. Do elements of your products or services make people live younger and longer?
2. If yes, how do you message this to your customers?
3. What holy grail products do you use?

---

[3] Vinita Mehta, PhD, EdM, "What Is It About Men and Breast Size?" *Psychology Today*, May 13, 2013; https://www.psychologytoday.com/us/blog/head-games/201305/what-is-it-about-men-and-breast-size.

8

Why Archetypes in Business Matter

↓

The structure of all archetypal stories alert us to *fear* and tell us how to reach *enlightenment*. Every organization needs to understand their customers' archetypal journeys or, as marketing executive Brad Davis simply states, why they exist. Once the organization understands the answer to this question, the leaders and their team need to map their company's own archetypal journey and figure out its story. This reveals a company's powerful purpose and galvanizes the corporate culture. Some call this a truthful and shared vision.

As I've worked with companies creating their own archetypal journey maps, watching the lightbulbs go on is always a rewarding experience. Instead of prolonging the process with a series of "kick-off" and exploratory sessions that rack up billable agency hours, we perform these one-day, continuous seven-hour journey maps with the people in an organization who touch the customer the most. Executives join the journey map, but the folks who talk to and meet with the customers, witnessing their journey, are given the stage. Every time we have mapped the archetype of the customer experience, we've found money. In other words, we've discovered a revenue driver that costs the organization nothing.

Although the details are confidential, we mapped a $1.5 billion organization through the eyes of customers looking to protect their assets from cyber fraud. This mapping profoundly changed the company's processes in addressing the emotional state of the customer right at the moment of onboarding. This simple but overlooked root messaging will save the organization millions in fraud prevention, and it established positive behavior from the onset of the relationship. The messaging was used in training and became a "suit of armor" that brought security to both the customer and the organization.

ARCHETYPAL PATTERNS THAT EXIST IN YOUR OWN LIFE

We're going to briefly step back from business for a moment to map an existing archetypal pattern in your own life. It is important to understand this because lasting business relationships and transactions are based on very personal human experiences. The customer's journey is the same as your personal journey. You are faced with enemies, allies, and tests of your own, and you seek to overcome fears and reach enlightenment. Let's look at mapping your customers' pain in the market the same way we "map" personal pain or ordeals you have endured.

First, think of an ordeal, a descent into the underworld you have endured, or a serious obstacle you have had to overcome in your life. It might be an illness, a death in the family, the loss of a job, or some other ordeal that dragged on for months. Look again at the Holmes and Rahe Stress Scale on page 5 and add up how many life stress units you endured during that period. Take a moment to recall the details, the time before the event, and the people surrounding the crisis. Then read each stage in the following mapping and answer these questions on a piece of paper.

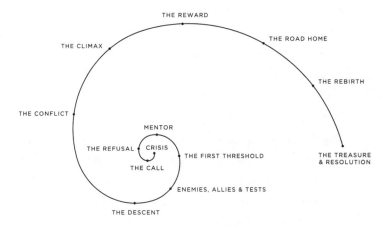

PERSONAL ARCHETYPAL JOURNEY

1. What was the crisis or ordeal?
2. Did you receive tragic news or was there a call to adventure that took you on a new course?
3. Did you resist this change or refuse this calling?
4. You sought out or discovered a friend or mentor who helped you. Who was this person?
5. Once you were encouraged by your mentor, you crossed a threshold and entered a new stage dealing with the crisis or ordeal. What was it?
6. After crossing this threshold, you encountered enemies, allies, and tests. Who and what were they?

7. After internal and external conflicts and tests with enemies, you approached a descent into the underworld, an abyss or a "dark night of the soul," where you felt completely alone. What did you do at that time?

8. The ordeal reached a decisive climax. What was it?

9. After a great battle, you overcame the crisis and basked in a reward. What was the reward?

10. You then pursued a road back to a life similar to where you were before the ordeal. Describe the journey.

11. Crossing another threshold, you experienced a rebirth, something that transformed you. What was the rebirth like?

12. You returned to your life with a treasure to benefit the ordinary world. This could be wisdom, money, a document, a newborn child, or the ringing of a bell at a children's cancer center. What was this treasure?

Whether you are aware of this or not, you are a hero on a journey rife with enemies, allies, and tests. As a hero, you either take action or fail to act on what drives your dreams and delivers you from your inmost cave. You will know you have completed this soul journey when you find yourself mentoring someone in their own ordeal who has sought you out. You will help them to overcome the ordeal and pain in their life.

The customer's journey and your own journey are much the same. This is clearly evident when working with founders and CEOs, because they are so closely connected to their own archetype; their hero's journey is fastened to every dimension of their organization.

For example, we worked with MIND Research Institute cofounder and chief R&D officer Matthew Peterson. He holds two PhDs and is the founder of ST Math, a computer program that has helped more than one million kids learn math visually, without using language. Using an animated penguin named JiJi, kids solve math puzzles that create a path from one side of a computer screen to the other side. Matthew's journey was overcoming his own dyslexia and mastering mathematics.

On the hero's journey, the most successful founders and CEOs often begin their battle with little or no weapons at all. The founders of Honda, Nordstrom, Apple, and countless others started with little or no money or resources. Domino's Pizza founder Tom Monaghan started with five hundred dollars of his own savings and a nine-hundred-dollar loan to buy a local pizzeria.

Over breakfast with Monaghan, I learned more about the foundations of Domino's and the company's quest for identity. Domino's original identity was a one-off local pizzeria named DomiNick's. Five years later Monaghan changed the name to Domino's, using the symbol, or logo, of a domino to identify their consistent method of selling pizza. Mona-ghan bought two more pizzerias and had three Domino's locations, symbolized by the three dots on the logo. The idea was to continue adding a dot for each new location, but new locations grew quickly and the three dots of the Domino's logo remain as a symbol of the original three locations.

Tom Monaghan was fearlessly consistent. In 1975, Domino's faced a dragon of its own in federal court when the makers of Domino sugar filed for infringement. Five years later, Domino's prevailed, defeated that dragon, and preserved the treasure of its brand equity.

In 2017, my friend Jeremy Renner's company produced a film called *The Founder*. The movie follows the life of Ray Kroc, the self-proclaimed founder of McDonald's fast-food restaurants. It's a direct depiction of Kroc's true life story told through an archetypal three-act structure. *The Founder* paints a picture of Kroc that is both inspiring and at times reprehensible, as he left his wife and went into a legal and psychological battle with the McDonald brothers.

The movie opens with Kroc as a struggling salesman on his own internal quest for identity, looking for a business to champion and grow. In the film, he meets the McDonald brothers, and with the weapons of a pen, personality, and grit, he goes on to franchise McDonald's restaurants across the United States. Kroc's archetypal journey is rife with enemies, allies, and tests, climaxing in the realization that despite all his suffering, hard work, and growth (his dragons and treasures), the McDonald brothers still have contractual control over him. Kroc takes a descent into the underworld and goes to war with Dick and Mac McDonald. He emerges with an epiphany from his CFO: Get into the real estate business and control the land that McDonald's restaurants are built on. Ultimately Kroc takes control of the McDonald's organization, proclaims himself the founder, and in 2004 through his wife, Joan, leaves $1.6 billion for the Salvation Army. Joan Kroc discovered her husband's true holy grail, his legacy on this earth—and it was greater than selling french fries.

The founder's journey is always a powerful and personal call to adventure, one the entire organization needs to fully understand to empower customers with identities and sharper swords to defeat dragons and capture the treasures that make the ordinary world an extraordinary one.

These are the five archetypes in the anatomy of yes. We will return to them in the third and final act of the book. From here, you are headed into the second act, filled with stories from the battlefields of business and rife with dragons, treasures, and adventures to discover how people get what they want.

YOUR QUEST FOR YES

1. What call to adventure have you currently answered?

Act II

Stories, Sales, and Your Quest for Yes

9

The Anatomy of a Great Presentation

↓

Good corporate presentations are research and sales results enveloped in a well-told story. There are lots of good presentations; their aim is to try to ingratiate the presenter, point praise at a team, or close a sale. *Great* presentations are very different; they follow the same construct of archetypal patterns. Great presentations are based on having a purpose that results in a call to action at the end of the meeting.

Let me tell you about my first great presentation. After I graduated college, my brother Jim and I started an advertising agency called Workhouse Corporation in Tempe, Arizona. A few days after my cross-country trek from New York, I began exploring the area, searching for a location for our new business. At the time my brother was working a full-time job as an engineer, and on the second day I arrived, I drove my rusted Volkswagen down an avenue named Mill, with old, historic buildings close to Arizona State University's Sun Devil Stadium.

One building in particular caught my eye, and I went inside to ask about office space. I had no real plan and less than a thousand bucks to my name. I walked up the stairs, knocked on the first door I saw, and was met by a wonderful lady named Judy. Within an hour we had worked out a deal in which I set up shop with a folding table and chair at the end of the hall in exchange for doing advertising work for her company. She also had three sons, two of whom I would hang out with at the office. Her son David was just starting to do stand-up comedy, and her other son was in advertising and engaged to a girl named Katie. Both boys later found success and are known today as comedian David Spade and Andy Spade, spouse of the late Kate Spade.

At this point, I needed work. I knew nothing about business, other than my experience as a paperboy, but I was obsessed with meeting people and was willing to work eighteen-hour days. I also knew the best way to get business is to go where the businesses are located.

Through tireless networking and preparation, my brother and I got a shot at pitching the Arizona State University sports advertising account, thanks to newly found friend and "ally." We sat in a conference room in Sun Devil Stadium, overlooking the football field, and presented a series of ads that elicited absolutely no positive reaction whatsoever from the athletic director and his marketing team. Within minutes our pitch was done, game over. As a last gasp, I got desperate and started asking questions.

I asked why people buy tickets to basketball games. The answers were "fast-paced, adrenaline-infused entertainment" and a "wild roller-coaster ride."

My brother and I looked at each other. I said, "Buckle up," and then suggested putting seat belt T-shirts on all the fans.

Those questions led to a conversation, the conversation led to a story, and the story led to a campaign for the Arizona State University basketball team called "Buckle Up." And that campaign led to Workhouse winning the account.

I learned a lot from that presentation. My most important takeaway was that presentations are stories—they require questions and interaction to be memorable and vault an idea into action.

A STORY WORTH TELLING

I've sat through hundreds of presentations—some of them good, many of them bad. I don't care if it's presenting the company's insurance plan, a new parking lot procedure, or the next great medical device, they are mostly awful because the presenters do not understand that the human mind craves the structure and adventure of a story. They fail to grasp that all information is best processed through crisis, conflict, and resolution. They don't understand ancient archetypes and the innate connection between fear and enlightenment.

An audience must care. You must raise the stakes in a way that engages your audience. Otherwise, there really is no need for a presentation or a meeting—you could have accomplished everything with an email or text message. Your presentations must have structure, and they must rise to the level of a story worth telling.

Whether your goal is a great meeting or a great presentation, open it with a question, then clearly state why you are meeting— outline the existing danger or issue (crisis) first, then explain the forces in play (conflict), and finally let your team or audience know what yes (resolution) will look like at the end of the meeting. If you're doing a visual presentation, do not fill a slide with more than twenty words—that's what printed materials are for.

Recall the speech given by Scottish revolutionary William Wallace in the film *Braveheart*. Wallace, played by Mel Gibson, opens his speech to an army of fellow Scotsmen who need direction. These soldiers don't know why they fight or what they are fighting for; they're just standing with weapons waiting for clear direction from their leaders. Wallace rides up and first states the goal of the meeting: "I see a whole army of my countrymen here in defiance of tyranny." He then asks a question about the conflict they are engaged in: "You've come to fight as free men... and free men you are. What will you do with that freedom? Will you fight?" and concludes the meeting with a compelling call to action: "They may take our lives, but they will never take our freedom!"

The preceding example may sound overly dramatic to someone preparing for a monthly finance meeting, but I challenge you to look at the agenda of your next meeting in this way:

Agenda for (date, time)

I. Opening question that states a long-term risk to the organization

II. State the goal of the meeting

III. State the crisis

IV. State the existing conflict

V. State the resolution the team will make before the meeting concludes

When building presentations and new product "pitch decks" for investors and companies, start with seven to twelve pages and collaboratively build a story with fewer than five words per page. Then create a distilled three-act story that brings the audience from a narrow understanding to whatever yes you are looking for.

Imagine a group of twelfth-century Samurai warriors, members of military nobility. In the age of the Japanese Samurai, grand tea ceremonies were held to create a focus for inner contemplation. These were held in a room with a door too small to allow men to enter with swords; it was a time to leave weapons at the door. The tea would take two hours to prepare. Imagine for a moment a meeting in your organization with no "swords" (i.e., smartphones, computers, paper, pencils).

We decided to hold a meeting like this at one company I worked with. We led a company-wide managers' meeting with more than one hundred attendees. We got rid of all the chairs and had everyone sit on the floor in a circle. We then passed out drums and tribal instruments for all to play, pound, and rattle instead of clapping. Several presenters held the "talking stick" as they addressed the managers, and dancers from a Native American center performed a spiritual dance and shared stories of their history and culture.

What was the importance of a meeting like this? We wanted to make certain that the managers left with the understanding that they are "on stage" every day, and that their words and talents impact every team member in the organization. And it worked. They all had a better understanding that when they spoke with their teams, they were tribal leaders with talking sticks, charged with hatching plans to protect and grow the tribe. Artful simulation and story are rocket fuel to a presentation or pitch.

The NTL Institute for Applied Behavioral Science would agree. Their research, conducted at the Rochester Institute of Technology, shows that audiences retain 5 percent of material through reading, 10 percent through lectures, and 78 percent through interaction and simulation. Think about how you learned to drive a car. The coursework and lectures on driving had little effect on your actual ability to drive a car. Taking the car out on the road, getting practical experience, and having someone teach you put skin on all those theoretical bones.

On another occasion, a client asked for our help with their annual sales meeting. They had a budget and a concept called "Walking in the Customer's Shoes." Simple enough. I had a friend at Vans, a world-renowned shoe brand, and we decided to make a custom pair of Vans shoes for every member of the company. Without giving away our plan, we surveyed employees and asked them a series of creative questions that inspired the design of the shoe. We worked with Steve Van Doren, whose father cofounded Vans, and he did an amazing job bringing the vision to light. We also called on some friends in the skate industry, who installed two large halfpipes at the venue, and we opened the event with two pro skaters doing a demo performance with a light show and pulsating music chosen by the skaters themselves. To make a big reveal, we had a giant wooden Vans shoe box made with a metal edge for the skaters to perform tricks on.

At the conclusion of the sales meeting, Van Doren stepped up on the giant shoe box, shared an inspiring story about community, and let every employee know that when they walk in their customers' shoes, they can also walk in a pair of Vans. At that moment, he stepped down and the giant shoe box was opened, revealing a custom pair of orange Vans designed specifically for our client's brand.

As with any great grassroots movement, the employees took it upon themselves to stage a competition between their departments as they circulated photos and videos on Instagram that creatively displayed their bright Vans.

YOUR QUEST FOR YES

1. Recall the last meeting you attended. Why were you there?
2. Did that meeting motivate or inspire you to do anything differently? If not, why? If yes, describe.

10

Values and Desires

↓

Think for a moment about everything around you as you read this book. Look at the shirt you're wearing and the chair you're sitting on. Notice things in your direct space that you've purchased. Every buying decision is based on the intersection of values and desires. This is true for your customers, and it is true for you personally. Your desires will intersect with your values in fulfilling those desires—these are the sacrifices you are willing to make to get what you want.

In advertising, we always position the customers' desires ahead of their values. This is why the archetypal story of your customers' desires is your most important message in marketing products and services. Every organization needs an internally aligned message architecture based on their customers' values and desires within all three dimensions of their business: (1) product superiority; (2) operational excellence; and (3) customer intimacy. Most successful organizations do two of these well, while a small percentage of world-class organizations excel at all three dimensions.

The clothes you are wearing right now and those hanging in your closet are an intersection of your values and desires (and have been influenced by your quest for identity). Clothing and fashion brands understand this well. Major luxury apparel brands know that they have customers who are heavy on cash and short on time. Luxe brands such as Prada, Dolce & Gabbana, and Versace will offer the most desirable, beautifully designed couture clothing for thousands of dollars per garment. Mid-tier fashion brands—Calvin Klein, Kenneth Cole, and Banana Republic—give people the fashion that they desire, but set the price dictated by their values. Discount fashion brands make clothes that look like luxe or mid-tier brands, but they compromise on some of the materials, design, and detailing because they know their customer is price-driven. Brands at this tier that do extremely well are H&M, Zara, and Chaps by Ralph Lauren.

Desires—what we want or crave—can only be truly measured in the brain. The human brain has a system of reward circuitry that guides and feeds our desires. This reward circuitry triggers the release of dopamine, a neurotransmitter that induces a pleasurable feeling. Because of this, there is a fine line between desire and addiction. This explains why you are addicted to the sound and vibration of a text message from your smartphone—a dose of dopamine is shot into your brain every time. Your text messages are very personal. Your emails are not as personal, so an alert that you have a new email is more likely to create anxiety. This is why 90 percent of all text messages in the United States are read in the first three minutes, as opposed to only 46 percent of all mobile emails.

Desires can be deceiving. The use of drugs to influence the reward circuit can lead a person to bypass survival activities and repeat the drug use (or abuse), because it is being rewarded over other activities. In fact, the reward circuitry in the brain that routes an addiction is the same system that routes feelings of intense and passionate love.

Human reproduction is one of the most powerful forces in the brain. Living organisms are wired and designed to reproduce. So, in the business of values and desires, let's look directly at human reproduction, or as *Psychology Today* describes this powerful desire: "It's why we're alive today and it's the first thing future generations depend on."[4]

As we look at reproduction, remember the Holmes and Rahe Stress Scale. The highest level of trauma we can experience as a human being is the death of a spouse or the death of a parent. The parent-child relationship and the desire to reproduce are the most powerful forces in the universe. Harnessing this compelling desire authentically and artfully is the most powerful force in sales.

AN ORGANIZATIONAL LOVE STORY

Advertising creatives often talk about storytelling and "brand love," but few apply the psychological "glue" of archetypal patterns and the construct of great love stories. Organizational love stories can be told by any company—from steel manufacturers and energy companies to technology and financial management groups. This does not mean we have to run ads telling people to love steel. The love story actually starts within the organization and the relationship it shares with its employees. This is where we do our organizational love story authoring and outline each

---

[4] "All About Sex," *Psychology Today*, https://www.psychologytoday.com/us/basics/sex.

chapter in the company's story. We start by looking at the company's products and services as though we were observing two teenagers in love. Instead of chasing customers like an overzealous young lad chasing a girl, we attract them through building the sales force's confidence in our brand and products. If the sales force is not in love with the product, the customer will not fall in love either.

Remember, every great love story is a retelling of the hero's willingness to break the boundaries of their own values to win over their beloved. From *A Midsummer Night's Dream*, *Romeo and Juliet*, and *Lancelot and Guinevere* to *Ghost*, *Slumdog Millionaire*, and *Twilight*, heroes have stretched the limits of their values to love and be with the person they desire.

Looking the part is also critical to the business of values and desires. Dental care brand Colgate once sold TV dinners. Smith & Wesson, a firearms manufacturer, sold bicycles, and Coors, a beer maker, came out with drinking water. These ventures all failed because we know these brands within their identities as dental hygiene, guns, and beer. When they branched out into different areas, they all suffered an identity crisis; they just didn't look the part.

This chapter is about values and desires, and the business of values and desires is discovering how far your customer will go to obtain your product or service. You can push the customer's values further if you can tap into their desires. If a brand reflects the fact that you've listened to your customers' desires, that brand will represent and stand for the customer. Your customers don't buy your product or service—they settle on the amount of money it will cost to attain their desires.

Whether you are seeking a yes from an individual or from an audience of customers, pay close attention to their desires. Play even closer attention to the elasticity of their values when it comes to achieving what they want. When we create compelling brand stories and campaigns in advertising, we create what the customer seeks to the point of making it an imaginary experience that the product will allow them to play out in real life.

At Disney Store, we tapped into the desires of children, whose imaginations have no bounds. We had to be open to images that lived beyond the clothing and toys we sold. My sketches, which we eventually photographed, were composed of elaborate images of children jumping into clouds in the shape of *Toy Story* character Buzz Lightyear. Another sketch was of a sleeping girl under stars that formed a constellation of Princess Jasmine and Aladdin on a magic carpet ride. To reach this customer, we had to dream as the cus-tomer and imagine the fantastic visions of children.

YOUR QUEST FOR YES
1. What does your customer desire most?
2. How far are your customers willing to go to purchase the products or service you offer?
3. What is your organization's love story?

11

Beggars and Choosers

↓

If you want something in life, don't be a beggar, be a chooser. Choosers have an inventory and abundance of assets that others want. Beggars want what choosers have. Beggars also wait to be chosen. Choosers decide whom they want to sell to, whom they want to work with, whom they want to love.

I had the good fortune to witness and learn all I needed to know about beggars and choosers when I lived in Venice Beach, California. This is a place where the wealthy play handball with the homeless and it is difficult to recognize who is who. Identifying the behaviors of beggars and choosers was far easier, and it had little to do with financial wealth.

At that time, in addition to working with a local ad agency, I had a talent agent who called me to audition for TV and movie roles. My days were a juggling act of acting and advertising. My car was full of clothes for the different characters I might audition for, and with no GPS in those days, like everyone else, I carried an inch-thick *Thomas Guide* map book that sat in my lap while I attempted to make calls on a flip phone. The really fun part was that these auditions were all over the city and suburbs of Los Angeles. Whoever did the city planning for greater Los Angeles must have been a maze creator. Movie studios, production companies, and casting directors are evenly scattered over a hundred-square-mile area riddled with out-of-state drivers, potholes, and bus stop benches featuring ads for bankruptcy and divorce.

I made very good friends in the entertainment business, many of whom continue to pursue their dream to this day, and a handful of whom have reached the top echelons of Hollywood.

The smartest people I know in Hollywood are the ones who created their own films—and their own destiny—with little or no budget. They didn't wait; they just took action. My friend of twenty-plus years, Jeremy Renner, is a master at this; he's a smart guy without a backup plan. He went through periods of saying no when it hurt the most. Jeremy said no because he never lost sight of why he came to Hollywood; his goal was to perform great characters in great films, not act in trendy TV shows. Saying no gets expensive, though—so expensive that he sacrificed basic needs for the ability to do so.

For months Jeremy and I had been writing a screenplay together called *Howl*. The Bravo Channel even filmed a short segment of us writing it. I had hit a stretch with no advertising clients and no acting work, and I had figured out a way to live on fifteen dollars a week (mostly thanks to ninety-nine-cent store-brand waffle mix). During this time, Jeremy got an audition for a film about serial killer Jeffrey Dahmer. He had just gotten back on his feet financially after taking a nighttime job; he wanted to keep his days open for auditions. After several callbacks, he got the lead in *Dahmer*.

The bad news was that it was a deferred-payment contract (translation: He wouldn't get paid until the film began making money). We talked about it over cheap whiskey. He accepted the call to adventure and took the role. Weeks later, I visited him on the movie set, and it was a bare-bones ordeal. No dressing rooms, no real meals, and only a Dixie cup of M&M's to snack on. He was lonely and hungry, but he loved what he was doing.

Months later, the film previewed in a small theater in Santa Monica. An agent from the William Morris talent agency saw it, found Jeremy on a Saturday, and signed him that Monday. For Jeremy, playing the role of Jeffrey Dahmer was an archetypal descent into the underworld. Within three months of descending into the abyss, he chose between starring roles in a movie called *The Big Bounce* and one called *S.W.A.T.* This is what I mean by a chooser outcome.

Another wise soul who defines the contrast between beggars and choosers is Dick Marconi. Dick and I meet for lunch once a month and talk about fearless pursuits, great art, and the slaying of dragons. He co-founded a multibillion-dollar nutrition company and later created an auto museum to house his collection of classic cars in Tustin, California; the museum has raised millions of dollars for children's charities.

I love the answers I get from asking Dick questions. I once asked him, "When you were a kid, what was the car you always dreamed of?"

He said, "Any car we could afford." I pressed him and asked why. "We never had anything," he replied. "If we got a pair of gloves or socks for Christmas, it was a great gift." Keep this in mind as I tell you the response I got from him when I asked, "What is the toughest and most valuable yes you ever achieved in life?"

Without a flinch, he answered: "I alway made sure that I was the yes."

This is the core divide between beggars and choosers. During the Depression, his father earned seven dollars a week working at a steel mill in Indiana, so Dick grew up with very little money. This could have easily made him a beggar instead of a chooser. When I asked him why he wasn't a beggar as a child, his response was, "To get what I wanted, I just had to look for the how."

On one occasion I asked Dick about how he pictured the holy grail of his legacy. He simply said, "To make the world a better place than how I found it." He lives these words in his charitable works, and he has made the world a better place in many ways. For instance, he was instrumental in restoring the *Pietà*, Michelangelo's sculpture that was severely damaged by a vandal with a rock hammer in 1972.

Beggars and choosers fundamentally look at transactions differently. A beggar chases customers and overpromises the value of a product. A chooser positions their product as an object of abundance that customers would be fortunate to own. Let's look at how beggars and choosers sell.

SELLING A PEN

In the movie *The Wolf of Wall Street*, Leonardo DiCaprio plays the role of convicted junk stock trader Jordan Belfort. In one scene, Belfort holds up a pen and says to his group of salesmen, "Sell me this pen." The exercise is designed to show how selling works. One of his cocky salespeople takes the pen from, him and says, "Write your name down on that napkin."

When Belfort tells him he doesn't have a pen, the salesman says, "Exactly. Supply and demand, my friend."

It's a nice story about a nice laissez-faire economics that might earn a buck—but would it create a customer for life? Does it form a relationship beyond the sale of the pen, and is there any purpose given to the pen other than a utilitarian one?

Let's look at how the sale of a pen is constructed in the anatomy of yes. It illustrates how a chooser behaves in service of others:

Salesperson: "Do you keep a journal?"

Customer: "No."
(Ninety-nine out of one hundred customers will say no. If they say yes, the script is not much different; it merely affirms what they know.)

Salesperson: "This might sound simplistic, but journaling is statistically proven to increase a person's success rate in achieving goals."

Customer: "OK. So what?"

Salesperson: "Well, is there a goal you have right now, personal or professional?"

Customer: "Yes, I want to lose fifteen pounds!"

Salesperson: "I can send you the study if you're interested, but the act of physically writing your goal on a piece of paper and sharing it with your family and friends activates a simple psychological principle. Using this pen and paper will give you a three-times better chance of achieving your goal."

Customer: "So you're saying that if I write down that I'll lose fifteen pounds, I will lose fifteen pounds?"

Salesperson: "Yes. Take this pen, write your goal, and share it with your friends and family. I know the power of writing and the power of pens; it's what I do for a living."
[Salesperson hands the pen to the customer.]

Salesperson: "This is a steel-point pen with a black lacquer body; it retails for twenty-nine dollars. And I want you to try it out for a week. If you don't like the pen, I'll take it back and cheer you on as you reach your goal."

Customer: "So I can have this pen for a week?"

Salesperson: "Yes, but only if you use this pen to handwrite a commitment to achieving a goal. If you don't like the pen, I'll take it back. As I mentioned, if you like the pen, I'd like twenty-nine dollars for it, and I'll give three dollars of that to your favorite charity. And you will lose fifteen pounds."

This transaction does not beg for a sale. Instead it creates a relationship based not only on utility but also on service. The pen is now endowed with personal qualities, statistics, and a story. And it does "good." The customer is more likely to share the story, show the pen, purchase the pen, and allow you to follow them on social media (this also opens up the customer's friends and family, which leads to future sales).

Get in the habit of asking yourself and your employees how your company "sells pens." Get people in the habit of saying yes to things they truly care about.

YOUR QUEST FOR YES

1. When does your organization act like a beggar?
2. When does your organization act like a chooser?
3. What do your customers need outside of the products and services you offer?

12

The Silent and Unfair Competitive Advantage

↓

Throughout high school and college, I wrestled. Wrestling is a great sport for teaching survival skills, as these athletes starve themselves to "make weight" and fight like two dogs in a barnyard while dehydrated. I wasn't a classic wrestler by any means; I was tall, lean, and built more for baseball. My silent and unfair competitive advantage over everyone in my weight class started with a method of running up and down twelve flights of granite stairs.

Every day our team ran for thirty minutes at the end of practice. Everyone hated the grueling adventure of running stairs—cold granite stairs straight up and down in the frigid temperatures of the Chicago suburbs in the winter. As we ran stairs, we were supposed to climb up and down without resting or even slowing our pace. There were closed doors at the landings between each flight of stairs. It was possible to exit these doors, rest, and get to a water fountain, but this was an unspoken cheat. I knew that if I didn't cheat, I'd have an advantage. To get that advantage I would never allow myself to stop. After a few months, I made an effort to lap everyone over the course of thirty minutes.

To get an even stronger advantage, I started hiding ankle weights under my sweatpants; this way no one would know I was training harder. This was one of the silent and unfair competitive advantages that put me on the varsity team by my sophomore year.

In the end, my wrestling career didn't amount to a deal with the UFC, but starving myself and creating more enduring, "silent" workouts taught me the discipline to land my first full-time job, going from a temp to earning six figures in six weeks. Here's how it happened.

SIX-FIGURE SILENT AND UNFAIR COMPETITIVE ADVANTAGE

Since the age of nine, I've had a job. Paper routes, a car-washing business, bussing tables at thirteen, working at a moving company, and other manual labor jobs. With my first company after college, I would create ads and campaigns for companies without them knowing it; this is called creative on "spec," or speculation. I would then go to the companies and show them the ads and a strategy that would make them more money. Besides the movies and TV shows, this was how I earned money. Fast-forward a few years, my wife and I found out we were having our first child, and we both thought a salaried job was more secure. I also walked away from the film business and we moved to my wife's home state of Minnesota to have our child. I soon learned Minnesotans don't really like Californians! After three months of pavement pounding I had no solid work prospects in Minnesota, so I applied for a job with a search engine company named Google. I heard from them pretty quickly, went through a series of phone interviews, and was offered an onsite interview in Mountain View, California. The interview was scheduled four months out and we were now open to leaving Minnesota for Northern California.

In the meantime, a recruiter back in California called me about a contract marketing position at a teen retailer named Wet Seal. The company did $500 million a year and was publicly traded, but sales were declining. My wife and I needed income, and with no prospects in Minnesota, I headed back to California alone to work at Wet Seal while we waited for Google. Within sixty days at Wet Seal, they offered me a six-figure job, and within four months we launched an e-commerce campaign that did a $2.6 million increase over the previous year's fourth quarter. The painful story behind that campaign was that it was entirely accomplished through creating silent and unfair competitive advantages.

My first day of contracting, Wet Seal gave me a pretty solid project. I really knew nothing about teen or luxury fashion, so I quickly needed to learn more about this niche and retail marketing than anyone in the organization.

It was simple. On lunch breaks, after work, and late into the night, I studied retail marketing and fashion. I went to where the customer was, online and at brick-and-mortar shopping malls. I created a vetting process for every competitive brand—I wanted to know what every competitor was doing: their offers, promotions, trends, marketing, press releases, and leadership. Next was to compile a "brand dissection" report for the team. Then I found a website, RagingBull.com, that showed how many shares the retail executives had, when they acquired them, and when they sold them, to gain insights about possible motivations behind their decisions.

I enjoyed the work, but from day one at Wet Seal, there was drama—lots of it. I kept quiet in a small office separate from most of it, but the vice president who hired me, someone I really liked, was soon fired by a new corporate officer. This executive came into the marketing department to "assess the damage." I had been there about a month, was essentially nobody, and she most likely considered me the temp. Luckily, I had been doing weeks of spec work on a campaign for their holiday season. I showed it to a few people in the department. They liked where it was going, and asked if we could all present it. The answer was yes, and we had two days to put the presentation together for the executive officers, CEO, merchandising team, and buyers.

The willing members of the marketing team rallied, and we put on a show complete with lighting, music, and three-dimensional displays. Most important, we included a two-inch-thick document containing an online survey of twenty-seven hundred of the brand's most faithful fans. We had created this survey in one day, sent it out to twenty thousand fans of the brand, and let them decide which campaign mantra to use. The new holiday campaign was titled "Get Gifted."

The presentation followed the archetypal construct of crisis (declining sales), conflict (competitors cutting into market share), and resolution (opening up the creative process to the brand's most loyal followers). The resolution was a bit like a magic show as we unveiled cool marketing piece after piece with popular music, trend elements, and a preview of the glamorous online experience that the customer could play out in the store. This was the output of all the lunches, nights, and early morning research. We achieved 100 percent buy-in through the customer survey; it was social proof: If their best customers said yes to the message, all customers would say yes. Although we received a relatively paltry marketing budget, they offered me a healthy six-figure salary with stock options.

LICKING THE SIDEWALKS

My silent and unfair competitive advantage at Wet Seal was hyper-focused research and knowing more about our competitors than anyone in the building. The same diligence can be focused on new business development. Whenever we present a new business strategy for regional businesses, I try to arrive a day early to understand their market. The exercise of "licking the sidewalks" begins by hitting the streets and intensely studying the people of the community. It is an adventurous silent and unfair competitive advantage.

The first step in licking the sidewalks is to stay at the "people's hotel," meaning not the most expensive and not the least expensive. I talk with the concierge first; they know the city best, and they know where the locals spend their time. I ask as many questions as I can to "crack the brand" and understand the connection between the company and the community culture. Then it's time to see the town; I go where the locals are, asking questions and baking their answers into my research and into the presentation.

For example, when we worked with Cox Communications, we licked the sidewalks by asking someone in Baton Rouge, Louisiana, what it would take for them to become a customer of Cox Communications. One woman told me it would take a call from Jacqui Vines (a well-known local personality in Baton Rouge and an executive at Cox). I asked the woman if we could share her story, took a picture of her, and got her phone number in case I could arrange for Jacqui to call her. I shared this in my presentation the next day, and the executives in Baton Rouge immediately asked for the woman's phone number so Jacqui could call her.

They wanted to understand why they were losing customers and how to get them back; we wanted their advertising business. Here's a key point that appears simple but is often forgotten: The only way to get what *I* needed was to get them what *they* most needed. We got business by doing what the other local agencies were not doing—this was our silent and unfair competitive advantage.

By the way, Ms. Vines did call that former customer and won back her business. This silent and unfair competitive advantage was a sharper sword needed to defeat a bigger dragon.

THE LONELY HOURS

The anatomy of yes can't be found sitting in your office chair. No amount of research, surveys, reports, or academia can substitute for "bare-knuckle" silent and unfair competitive advantages, licking the sidewalks, and embracing the artful act of discovering your customers' archetypal journey. If you quietly put in the hard work and do your own competitive analysis, walk the stores, dissect online competitors, talk with people (not just your neighbor's kids), and at the opportune moment put that knowledge into action, you will increase your chances of a successful campaign by 1,000 percent. Most people just don't want to do it.

If you are fearful of this strategy massively failing and getting fired for it, you're on the right track. Your life is a rare collection of failures and successes. Every great call to adventure you accept, every dragon you slay, and every test you fail are all compounded into the *story of you*. As Alexandre Dumas wrote, "Life is a storm, my young friend. You will bask in the sunlight one moment, be shattered on the rocks the next. What makes you a man is what you do when that storm comes."

Dumas' words are reflected in the words of Kevin Caroll, the former chief officer of play at ESPN and Nike. Kevin told me, "Champions are made in the lonely hours." Make plans for your lonely hours, have a secret unfair competitive advantage, and get ready, there's another storm coming.

People you work with have descended into many organizational underworlds, and they help the organization endure the storms and grow the company. If you have read this far in the book, it's likely that you are one of those individuals. The more you do this, the more you will lead people.

In the next chapter, we'll look at heroes: leaders who take great personal risks to grow a company to the point where the lines between vision and delusion are blurred.

YOUR QUEST FOR YES

1. Do you have a silent and unfair competitive advantage? Describe it here.
2. When was the last time you licked the sidewalks and dissected the competition? Describe your experience.
3. What plans do you have for your lonely hours? How willing are you to pay the price?

13

Why We Say Yes to Functionally Delusional People

↓

We are fascinated with delusional people. We will often follow them, watch for what they will do next, and even say yes to them when we would never have expected to. A truly delusional person is not hallucinating, under the influence of drugs, or experiencing a mood disorder; they are living out their beliefs in real time. Fear and common sense are what keep us from doing the same. Delusional people are not schizophrenic, nor is there a correlation with IQ. We can refer to them as functionally delusional (as opposed to clinically delusional). They can be highly successful in life and in business. There are many among us.

Neuroscientist Phil Corlett of Yale University explains that typical delusions include inflated ideas about oneself. This doesn't mean delusional people are narcissists or are egotistical; instead they are directly living through their own belief system. According to Corlett, "Beliefs form in order to minimize our surprise about the world. Our expectations override what we actually see."[5] Delusional people have very high expectations of

---

[5] Phil Corlett, quoted in Tanya Lewis, "Delusional People See the World Through Their Mind's Eye," LiveScience, August 20, 2013, https://www.livescience.com/39038-how-delusions-shape-perception.html.

the world and of themselves. Is this a belief and behavior system different from that of people we regard as visionaries?

The real difference between a delusional person and a visionary is the difference between an expectation and a vision. If you expect the impossible to happen, sometimes it will, but often it won't. This is why we watch YouTube videos of people attempting crazy stunts—they expect them to work. If you're playing along here, we are giving value to delusion as a catalyst for achievement. So let's look at a list of potential innovators, risk takers, and pioneers whom many have followed and see if they are delusional or visionary:

- Evel Knievel, motorcycle stunt performer
- Jackie Joyner-Kersee, Olympic track and field gold medalist
- Robert Goddard, inventor of the liquid-fuel rocket

EVEL KNIEVEL

As a young man, Robert Craig Knievel Jr. was fired from a mining company for performing a wheelie with an earth mover, ultimately driving the earth mover into the city's main power line and leaving Butte, Montana, without electricity for several hours. Crazy, eh? He later played semiprofessional hockey and convinced the Czech Olympic hockey team to play an exhibition game against his home team, the Butte Bombers. Bobby was also a US Army veteran, and lived by a consistent code of conduct, preaching antidrug messages to kids at his events. He always followed through on his word, saying, "When you give your word to somebody that you're going to do something, you've gotta do it." When Bobby Knievel said he was going to jump nineteen cars, he did. When the US government told him he could not jump the Grand Canyon in a rocket, he jumped Snake River Canyon.

During Evel Knievel's career, the Ideal Toy Company sold more than $125 million in action figures, outfits, and their number-one selling toy, the Evil Knievel stunt cycle. Knievel's career crossed all five archetypes, beginning with his identity—the changing of his name from Bobby to Evel, and the superhero's costume and cape. Every jump and challenge was a dragon to slay, and his shiny weapon was a Harley-Davidson XR-750 motorcycle. Knievel's many descents into the underworld cost him more than thirty-five broken bones, thirty-six months in the hospital, and a blood transfusion that gave him hepatitis C, eventually leading to his death. His restoration of the wasteland was carried out in the many charities he raised money for, his message to kids about drugs, and his push for mandatory motorcycle helmet laws. Knievel's holy grail is a legacy of stories, motorcycle records, a religious conversion, and a funeral eulogy from actor Matthew McConaughey. Was Evel Knievel delusional or visionary?

JACKIE JOYNER-KERSEE

At eighteen, Jackie Joyner-Kersee was diagnosed with an asthma condition that landed her in the emergency room several times and eventually led to a near-fatal asthma attack. She recovered from the attack and went on to become a six-time Olympic medalist, with three golds, one silver, and two bronze; and to be named by *Sports Illustrated* as the greatest female athlete of the twentieth century. Joyner-Kersee's hero's journey crossed all five archetypes as well, starting with her early years in East St. Louis, Illinois. Inspired by a TV movie about female athlete Babe Didrikson Zaharias, Joyner-Kersee set out to become a multisport athlete, achieving a heptathlon world record that stands today, and she is still ranked among the top twenty-five female college basketball players.

Jackie Joyner-Kersee's legacy lives on through her philanthropic work, and in repeating the archetypal story from Babe Didrikson Zaharias. In the same way she was inspired by Zaharias, she has inspired countless other athletes to overcome obstacles and achieve greatness. Was Jackie Joyner-Kersee delusional or visionary?

ROBERT GODDARD

Robert Goddard, the founding father of modern rocketry, became interested in space after reading a book titled *The War of the Worlds*. At the age of seventeen, he climbed a cherry tree and later wrote about his epiphany:

> On this day I climbed a tall cherry tree at the back of the barn . . . and as I looked toward the fields at the east, I imagined how wonderful it would be to make some device which had even the possibility of ascending to Mars, and how it would look on a small scale, if sent up from the meadow at my feet . . . I was a different boy when I descended the tree from when I ascended. Existence, at last, had purpose.[6]

Goddard's accomplishments are legendary, including creating the first liquid-fueled rocket, which was successfully tested

---

[6] Milton Lehman, *This High Man: The Life of Robert H. Goddard* (New York: Farrar, Strauss, and Co., 1963).

in 1926, and receiving both a Congressional Gold Medal and a Daniel Guggenheim Medal (awarded for engineering). Despite this, Goddard was ridiculed by the press for his theories and his visions of spaceflight. The press badg-ered him until he ran into hiding, keeping his theories and writing private.

Would young Robert Goddard be seen as delusional or visionary?

Think about the Wright brothers, Thomas Edison, Emily Dickinson, Marie Curie, Michael Jordan, Chuck Yeager, "Macho Man" Randy Savage, and Patricia Bath, who despite growing up in poverty, worked her way through medical school and later invented a device that transformed cataract surgery. How many thought these people were delusional before they succeeded?

Whether we think they were delusional or visionary, we observe people like this intently. We want to watch them try it first, whatever *it* is. We want to follow people who are going to attempt the impossible. We either rally behind them or hope they fail. We want to witness the hero's journey before we go out and try slaying a dragon of our own. We say yes to the functionally *delusional* because they are delusional enough to push the boundaries of what is possible, and *functional* enough to see it through. This is crossing the threshold from delusional to visionary.

A BUSINESS OF PEOPLE

Functionally delusional people are vital to the growth and success of your organization. They will test and expand the universe of what can be accomplished. They can also be a pain in the ass. Do not dismiss these people, especially if they are the founder or CEO of the company. The functionally delusional are most effective when questioned. They have little patience for people who don't see how easy it looks to them. Asking them smart and systematic questions will help them connect the dots of a plan, drawing out the functional steps to accomplish the impossible. The functionally delusional are almost always what I call "deliberate creators."

A deliberate creator's world is full of barriers, challenges, and ordeals, and the world doesn't really care. But they are the polar opposite of a victim. When I use the word *victim*, I'm not referring to true victims of crimes and abuses; rather, I'm describing a mental state that holds people back from advancing their lives and the lives of others. These victims focus on unfair circumstances, and they see the fact that they have been abused, wronged, cheated, and betrayed as the reason they have not succeeded.

Deliberate creators see the world only as they envision it. They ignore their past and instead choose to dominate the day. Most people fall somewhere in the middle of this scale and move to either side throughout their lives; few are true deliberate creators. You can recognize a deliberate creator—they are functionally delusional in the way they take control of their lives despite everything stacked against them. Victims, on the other hand, expect failure and use it as an excuse for their lack of success.

Have you ever imagined your funeral and only a few people in your life standing over your coffin? It probably was during a moment of self-pity. At that moment, you were living a victim's dream. On the other hand, in the most joyful and victorious moments of your life, you do not imagine your funeral. You're not focusing on yourself or the future; instead you are filled with the adrenaline of the moment, and life moves effortlessly in slow motion. These are the magical moments when you've found your yes.

HOW A DELIBERATE CREATOR SAVED MY LIFE

A few years ago, my buddy Russell Kuchynka called me out of the blue and said he had an open permit to climb Mount Whitney, and since one of his friends had canceled, he was looking for someone to join the adventure. It would be a one-day, twenty-two-mile, seventeen-hour, straight up and straight down climb and descent. I worked late into the night before the day of the trip to Lone Pine, California.

The plan was to start at the base of Mount Whitney at midnight on Sunday, climb with headlamps, and reach the 14,505-foot summit at sunrise, around 6:00 a.m. We would then hightail it back down the mountain and make it back in time for work on Monday.

I tried sleeping before 9:00 p.m., with no luck. We hit the trail and set off into the black of night. At 4:00 a.m., around 11,000 feet, the combination of altitude sickness and lack of sleep put my head in a vise. Then the hallucinations started. I was seeing monster faces in the rocks, and when I pointed my headlamp at large blocks of granite, I saw what looked like hieroglyphics. As long as I knew it was a hallucination, I was OK. At one point I sat down, thinking I could sleep for fifteen minutes and then continue climbing. (In case you decide to try, it doesn't work—keep climbing.)

As I sat on the ground in 15-degree temperatures in the midst of high winds and hail, I thought about another friend, Nehemiah Papalii. I worked with Nehemiah at Goodwill. He had been born with multiple birth defects and deformities and had endured more than ten experimental surgeries to remedy his conditions. Nehemiah was not supposed to have lived past the age of seven; he was twenty-six at the time. He told me, "I wake up every day in pain and go to sleep every day in pain. Coming to work and being the best is what gets me out of bed."

I made it to the summit with Nehemiah's face ahead of me every step I took. At 6:30 a.m. with altitude sickness, dry heaves, and very little body heat, I reached the summit to see the sunrise, and then Russell and I sprinted back down to lower altitudes. I truly believe Nehemiah saved my life, though he doesn't know it. Nehemiah Papalii was a deliberate creator.

WHY THE FUNCTIONALLY DELUSIONAL MATTER

If you can be delusional enough to expect the impossible, yet functional enough to execute a plan, you will achieve great things. You will also inspire many people to beat their fears and achieve great things themselves. When we look at Myers-Briggs personality types, the Visionary/Confidant/Dreamer is the rarest, while Protector/Overseer/Supporter is the most common. When comparing these two personality types, we see that Protectors closely follow Visionaries and Dreamers, just as readers follow heroes in stories who go on daring adventures.

YOUR QUEST FOR YES

1. Do your company's products or services challenge your customers to achieve the impossible?

2. Who showed you that it's OK to try the impossible? How did they do this?

3. See if you can think of some other examples of functionally delusional individuals or deliberate creators. What sets them apart from everyone else?

14

The Biggest Buys

In this chapter I'll share what I've learned through working with banks, loan officers, and realty groups. Essentially, the bigger the buy, the bigger the battle. The buying and selling of a home is the most anxiety-ridden transaction we endure; it is one of the few purchases that address both a base need (shelter) and the greatest level of achievement (self-actualization).

This story starts in 2007. The housing market in Southern California was booming. My wife, Ellen, and I were shopping for houses in Orange County, California. We discovered that even zero-lot-line houses were going for about five hundred dollars a square foot, and we decided we were not going to buy. Instead we decided to lease, but we continued to look at houses for sale on the weekends, trying to get a read on the market. We ended up leasing until 2010, when we were due to have our second child. The housing market was no longer booming; in fact, it was just about at the height of the housing meltdown.

Everyone told us it was a great time to buy. The housing crash had taken prices down, and there was lots of inventory. We got in touch with a Realtor and began looking at five to ten homes each weekend. We quickly learned that the market was flooded with houses no one wanted—short sales, abandoned foreclosures in serious disrepair, and over-priced fixer-uppers. And each time a desirable home came on the market, we made an offer that seemed to go into a black hole; we seldom heard back whether it was accepted, and when we did, the story was always the same: The house went to a cash buyer. It was a simple equation; even though we were "A-paper" buyers through our bank, a Realtor could close a sale with a cash buyer quicker and with less risk of the deal falling apart.

In the book *Freakonomics*, authors Steven D. Levitt and Stephen J. Dubner expertly dissect the hidden side of incentives and transactions and explore the motivations of Realtors. I had read the book three years earlier and wasn't happy about what it said about those motivations.

The listing agent (the Realtor who is representing the seller) typically earns a 3 percent commission. The buyer's agent also earns a 3 percent commission for bringing the buyer. Although this looks like a simple equation, the listing agent representing the seller has all the power. They are able to position one offer to the seller over another. Obviously, if the listing agent receives a cash offer, there is less risk and less time to close the sale, and likely a less emotionally invested buyer, who requires minimal hand-holding through the process.

Our search went on, and we gained new information about the process with every failure. At one point, I realized our offers might never get in front of the seller, so I researched the bank that was holding the existing loan and faxed our offer and bank qualifications directly to them. No luck. I battled back and forth through our Realtor with a listing agent who wouldn't return phone calls. The frustration was mounting, and our second child was due in three months. We wanted to be in a home—our own home.

This is when I started researching the behavior of cash buyers. Most of them were heavy on cash and short on time. For the most part, cash buyers were not physically visiting these homes; instead they looked at key indicators and made offers as investments. They did, however, have agents working on their behalf to vet the properties and process the transactions. These Realtors were working with the listing agents who represented the sellers.

After seeing more than a hundred homes and experiencing multiple failures, we started to figure out how to beat a cash buyer. We stopped working with our own Realtor and offered the listing agent the one advantage we had over cash buyers: The listing agent could double their commission by cutting out the buyer's agent. Instead of only earning 3 percent, the listing agent could earn 6 percent on the sale of the home. Remember, the listing agent has all the power.

Even still, the process was not perfect. If we saw a property listed with a realty company, it wasn't safe. If another Realtor between them handled our phone call, they could stand to get a piece of the commission. Through the series of defeats we experienced, we were able to fully learn the process.

It went like this: We had a set of parameters for homes in certain price ranges, neighborhoods, and square footage set to alert my smartphone the moment they came on the market. If it looked right, we immediately called the listing agent for the property. If someone else answered the phone, we would say, "I would like to speak with the listing agent for [123 Main Street]." If they responded, "I am working on that property," or something of that nature, we would reply, "I would like to speak with the listing agent only."

Next, if the home fit within our parameters, we would make an offer sight unseen—much like a cash buyer. We would then say, "We will email you our qualification information from the bank, and we do not have a Realtor."

There was usually a pause. The Realtor might ask, "Did you want to see the property?"

The answer was, "Eventually, but please present our offer to the seller. We will send you our qualification letter from the bank."

We were behaving like cash buyers, not overly interested in seeing the home first, disinterested in the details of the home, and creating an opportunity that was more profitable than a cash buyer. When we toured the home, we once again behaved like cash buyers. Instead of commenting on what we liked, we pointed out everything we didn't—this is how cash buyers begin negotiations. Once we figured out this piece of the puzzle, we were in escrow on a home within three weeks with very reputable and ethical Realtors who served us well all the way through closing and the hand-off of the keys.

Everything we learned through the process came through accepting the simple fact that life is unfair—and business can be even more unfair. Once we accepted that fact, we got busy thinking like deliberate creators, searching for our silent and unfair competitive advantage.

The one common thread that the top producers all share is that they authentically serve more to sell more. Great Realtors do what apps and websites cannot do; they courageously lead their clients along a road map that avoids the painful traps of buying and selling homes and provides an experience that protects them from the highest levels of anxiety in the process.

Let's dig deeper into homes—your future home—and discover the anatomy of yes in one of the most defining purchases of your life.

ALWAYS HOME

As we alluded to in the opening of this chapter, home buying is the only purchase you will make that hits at both the top and bottom of Maslow's hierarchy of needs. At the bottom and most basic needs, a home is shelter and necessary for survival. At the top of the hierarchy, a home is a person's castle, a reflection of who they are and an expression of self-actualization.

When my company worked with a bank client in home mortgage strategy and advertising, we first spoke to who touched the customer the most: the loan consultants. We identified home buyer profiles and matched those with research I had done years earlier for a home improvement reality show. We focused on four specific types of home buyers:

- **Homebodies:** These are home buyers looking for comfort. They are less interested in location, style, and size; they want comfort and simplicity.
- **Fixer-Uppers:** These buyers are DIY couples who enjoy running multiple trips to home improvement stores on the weekends to upgrade and fix their own houses.
- **Entertainers:** These are couples who love to entertain guests and show off their fancy appliances and open-floor-plan gourmet kitchens.

- **Castle Keepers:** These buyers are wealthy folks who will go out of their way, even impractically, to improve their home with exotic appliances, artwork, and stonework from far-off lands.

Identifying these psychographics helps us understand the quest for these identities, and this knowledge is needed to understand what drives the home buyer decision process. Understanding the desires and intentions of the buyer will dictate the sales strategy; for instance, a Fixer-Upper and an Entertainer will have a greater propensity to DIY their mortgage online, a Homebody is more likely to visit their local bank or credit union, and a Castle Keeper is more apt to pay cash or use their trusted lending institution.

We next looked at the competitors in the home mortgage space, especially Rocket Mortgage, which was spending a fistful of cash on advertising. One key strategy was for the bank to drive more value to Realtors by listening to their needs and creating financial products that reflected what the current climate's customers wanted. Realtors had what the bank did not—the day-to-day emotional connection with the customer. Within six months, there was a 67 percent increase in mortgages with one realty group alone. The best part was that it cost nearly nothing in hard costs; all it needed was big brains, relationships, and staying obsessed with what the specific customer psychographic desired.

One of the by-products we learned through the process was that there is a story in every home. This strategy starts with what is called a listing presentation. This is the *Shark Tank*–like competition for the owner of a home to list their home with a real estate agent. Agents meet with homeowners and mostly talk about how great they are through sharing their stats, successes, personality, and promises. We looked at it differently. Instead, we ask the owner truthful questions about their home in a quest to understand the moments of joy they've had in it. This becomes a "love story." This love story is told to the buyers who are looking *not* for a home, but for the same joy and a love story of their own.

As for the archetypal journey of Realtors themselves, very few understand the power of their own identity. Many Realtors choose to market a photograph of themselves from decades earlier and broadcast it on every printed surface they can find. There is some value to frequency in marketing, but it's a dangerous strategy if not positioned well. A Realtor's brand is no different than that of professional athletes such as LeBron James and Serena Williams. These are two top-performing athletes who have personally branded athletic shoes created by their parent brand, Nike.

The best real estate agents are those who understand this balance and brand themselves exactly in the manner politicians get elected. And yes, it actually is a popularity contest, but the contest is based on reputation, which is the aggregate value of a personal or corporate brand. We'll talk about politicians and the anatomy of yes in the next chapter.

YOUR QUEST FOR YES

1. Do you have a personal brand?
2. Do you serve more to sell more?

15

Build a Wall with Hope and Change, Because It's the Economy, Stupid

↓

We're Going to Build a Wall . . . Hope and Change . . . It's the Economy, Stupid. Do these phrases ring a bell? They are combinations of words that helped moved a nation to elect various candidates, all words that reflect the values and desires of a populace.

In April 2016, six months before the US presidential election, I gave a talk at California State University, Fullerton. During my talk I said that Donald Trump would win the presidential election based solely on his business and marketing strategy.

I have read scores of opinions on why the election resulted in a Trump victory, but it was very obvious he would prevail when you looked at three key indicators: audience, ads, and rallies. When I say ads, I don't mean the ads that Clinton and Trump were airing on TV or online; I'm referring to the ads people were using to represent their candidate—specifically on social media, on their front lawns, and on bumper stickers.

Southern California, where I live, is a strong Democrat region. In the year leading up to the election, something just didn't look right. In 2008 and 2012, there were Barack Obama HOPE AND CHANGE signs and bumper stickers everywhere. In 2008 there was also the iconic red, white, and blue Shepard Fairey illustration of Obama on the pages and profiles of millions of social media accounts. Along with signs and bumper stickers, these are a qualitative indication that the audience is wearing the candidate's brand, much like a football fan wears a player's jersey. This could be a silly measuring stick, but more important were the "ads" coming from the general populace in 2016, not from the candidates, that told me the polls and prediction data were off.

Then there were the rallies. Trump was doing two, sometimes three a day in swing states. The rallies were attracting 5,000 to 30,000 attendees, depending what source was reporting. Let's settle on 10,000 a rally at an average of 1.5 per day, 5 days per week—that's 75,000 attendees a week. Let's take out the viral coefficient of influence and just look at attendees. If just 20 percent of these attendees voted in addition to paying for a ticket, that's converting 15,000 votes in a 5-day week. Trump was campaigning every week. The gross number of attendees at these rallies also told me the data were wrong. Note, these are the same persistent and consistent, ground-and-pound campaign strategies we preach to companies. It takes ninety days to build marketing pressure, and if a campaign is paused or redirected, it will take another ninety days to rebuild the pressure.

The Hillary Clinton campaign spent over $1 billion, much of it on advertising. Comparatively, the Trump campaign spent less than $15 million on advertising, but through publicity it achieved an estimated $2 billion in earned media. Remember, brands are built on publicity, not advertising.

Manic as it may have seemed, Trump and his team intimately understood message architecture, publicity, and marketing. They also masterfully used Twitter to go directly to the people, circumventing advertising spend and compounding the reach through publicized retweets on Twitter, digital media, and even traditional media. I saw precisely what he was doing with every tweet, every insult, and every proclamation. In this University talk, I shared that one of the reasons Trump would win was because he used these mantras and visual hammers in combination. Here's a quote from an article about that talk:

> [Burke] talked about how Republican presidential candidate Donald Trump knows marketing and media and that he is doing things in his campaign that a lot of companies don't do.

> Burke stated, "[First off] he has a visual hammer. A visual hammer is something you see all the time, and it's his hair . . . that is his identifying mark. The second thing he does is he understands mantras. What he is saying with his mantra is 'Build a wall, build a wall, build a wall' . . . he knows that they work."[7]

THE MEANING OF MANTRA

The word *mantra* has several meanings, originating in one of the first languages, Sanskrit, to describe a repeated sound with psychological and spiritual powers. In the anatomy of yes, a mantra brings simple clarity through a repeated phrase that catapults a customer into action. This is not a slogan or a tagline. A mantra is an artful command, a rallying cry proclaimed by a brand to its army of faithful followers. Creating mantras takes no less than

---

[7] Brent Cabatan, "Former Brand Director of Disney and Wet Seal Shares His Insights into the Competitive Field of Marketing," *Daily Titan*, April 6, 2016, https://dailytitan.com/2016/04/former-brand-director-of-disney-and-wet-seal-shares-his-insights-into-the-competitive-field-of-marketing/.

thirty days and no more than sixty. I have loved writing these three-to-five-word stories. For DisneyStore.com: "Shop with the Mouse"; Goodwill: "Find the Good"; and when we did battle with AT&T and DirecTV, we repeatedly exclaimed, "Cox Crushes the Competition." These all seem like simple phrases, but each was orchestrated with a visual symbol that was immediately recognizable to customers. All these campaigns delivered record sales and two of them won both regional and national awards.

All this brings us back to the title of this chapter. Was it the three words "Hope and Change" that won it for Obama? "It's the Economy, Stupid" for Bill Clinton? "Build a Wall" or "Make America Great Again" for Trump?

As a writer and connoisseur of three-word mantras, I know this: If you can capture the frequency of a community and artfully express their values and desires in three to five words, you'll create a harmonizing anthem that is more powerful than a jingle and more immediately identifiable than a Billboard top-ten song.

Conversely, if you come up with an artful combination of three words and spend a massive amount of ad dollars pushing it to a community, you'll end up wasting those ad dollars unless you first leave the castle, lick the sidewalks, and immerse yourself in that community's values and desires.

A MANTRA MISFIRE

A few years back I came up with an incredible three-word campaign for a client. There was no trademark on it, and we got goose bumps every time we heard it. We kept it quiet while we applied for a trademark and even bought the URL. Next, we tested the mantra in a mix of other statements through online focus groups and surveys with employees. To our dismay, the specific audience we were targeting didn't like the three-word mantra that we personally loved. As an ad guy, even knowing it was a winner, I had to let it go because it didn't reflect the community—it just sounded like it did.

When you get a mantra harmonized, it will take on an emotional and transactional life of its own. I call this an "emotional thermodynamic." If you hear marketing and advertising professionals use phrases like, "We need an authentic message," or "We need a viral video," run from them. An authentic message cannot be created. A viral video cannot be filmed. Authenticity and the viral sharing of products, services, brands, and organizations are the result of telling a consistent and honest story. Customers instinctually know if you are lying.

THE VISUAL HAMMER

A visual hammer is exactly what it sounds like. Hit people hard with an extremely identifiable visual image, and do it frequently. Author Laura Ries wrote the book "Visual Hammer" about the emotional power of visuals. In the book, Ries illustrates how visual hammers are not merely a trademark, but the essence of a brand communicated through a visual, not words.

According to advertising legend David Ogilvy, a brand is "the intangible sum of a product's attributes: its name, packaging, and price, its history, its reputation, and the way it's advertised." All of that can be represented by a single symbol or visual. Many famous people have a visual hammer that makes them identifiable. In the following list of influential people, what is the first thing that comes to mind when you read the names?

· Winston Churchill
· Abraham Lincoln
· Mother Teresa
· Fidel Castro
· Humphrey Bogart
· Bono of U2

If you saw a top hat, a beard, a white-and-blue habit, a military cap, a fedora, and a pair of dark sunglasses, you identified them by their visual hammer. Visual hammers are critical to brand building and differentiation, especially with public figures. But the visual hammer alone is useless without a synchronized mantra. Commit to consistently using a visual hammer and a mantra in combination and you will be employing the strategy and the behavior of world-class brands.

THE BOOMERANG ARCHETYPE

What is a boomerang for? I ask this question of many business groups. The answer is always, "For hunting." My next question is, "How do you kill something with a boomerang?" I hear many different theories, such as "You throw it at a bird and it comes back." Boomerangs are for hunting, but a boomerang is not a weapon. Understanding the methodology of a boomerang is understanding the methodology of using disruption to get what you want.

I spent three weeks adventuring in Australia, from Sydney to Cairns. I met a historian while looking for an authentic boomerang to bring back to the states. He told me the story of how boomerangs really work. I learned that there are two distinct types: ones that fly and return and ones that don't.

Using boomerangs, the first disruptive marketing campaign was launched fifteen hundred years ago by the Aborigines on the Australian outback. It worked like this.

An Aboriginal hunter shaped a piece of wood into an aerodynamic airfoil designed to travel in a triangular path, returning to the hunter. This "flying stick" was only intended to distract or disrupt the prey; to the prey the boomerang looked and sounded like a strange bird in the sky. This disruption caused the prey to stop and stare; it caught their eye exactly like billboards, TV ads, and even blimps are designed to do for people. The messages that these mediums deliver are the "kylies"—the boomerangs that don't fly and return. These boomerangs are used to bludgeon the prey. This might be a rather raw explanation of advertising, of getting someone to a yes, but it is a great metaphor for the messages businesses today are sending.

Think of your own company. What messages are you sending that disrupt and get the attention of your intended audience? Once you have sent that disruption, is your brand name and mark glued to that disruption? This is an effective short-term strategy, but be cautious not to bludgeon your audience with too many deadly "kylies"; instead use disruption to send unexpected moments to your customer. These unexpected moments are no different from the unexpected gifts and wishes we give to our friends, family, and lifelong relationships. Desirable disruption can be magical.

YOUR QUEST FOR YES

1. What is your company's visual hammer?
2. What is your company's mantra? (Ideally this must be a two-to-five-word command that begins with an action verb.)
3. What desirable disruption can you create?

16

Get More Yes on the Internet

↓

There is a company that is a master at getting a yes online: Amazon.com. It's a company whose archetypal journey started as a restoration of the wasteland, curating a massive collection of unused books (knowledge and entertainment) and connecting them to buyers (knowledge and entertainment seekers). Amazon is no longer primarily a book company, or even a product company. Amazon is in the business of operational excellence and customer experience—it's what the company does best. They truly arm every customer, as a hero, with the tools, weapons, and resources to do battle every day, restore wastelands every day, and find identity and even products that promise the holy grail. This is why Amazon is so powerful. Imagine Sir Lancelot ordering replacement parts for his armor and a new sword on Amazon Prime, delivered the same day by a drone right to the battle-field, thirty minutes before war.

Amazon runs its business online, and without the advent of the internet, the organization would not exist as it does. As such, this is a company that has mastered the art and science of getting a yes on the world wide web. We are going to disassemble the online purchasing process and find the anatomy of yes online.

THE ONLINE DECISION-MAKING PROCESS

Now let's focus on how the mind interprets emotions and transactions using computers and smartphones. The sum of this knowledge is for another book, but I'd like to share some stories about the online decision-making process. Remember, decisions are based on values and desires, and getting a yes over a smartphone or computer is very different from doing so in person.

First, we have to take a step back in time. Before televisions existed, people used the radio. Radio is not an interactive media; there was a volume dial and a station or frequency dial. It was a world where the spoken words from people anywhere in the world came through a little box. There was no way to have a conversation with a standard radio receiver.

Then came television. Now images, people, and sounds, eventually from anywhere in the world, could be seen and heard—simple stuff. Next came *Pong*. It was a harmless little console video game that debuted in 1975. The game came from a company named Atari, who began the first true interaction with television.

Let's move ahead just five years to 1980. Internet protocols were being used by academia, by the military, and within corporations (which called it the "intranet"). By 1995 the internet had exploded and was reaching one-third of the total world population; it's been said that the internet is the eighth continent.

In 2004, a video recorded by a teenage vlogger in New Jersey changed the world by transforming how we interpret information on the internet as well as how we transact on the internet. The teenager, Gary Brolsma, created a video known as the "Numa Numa Dance." It was named after the song "Dragostea Din Tei," performed by O-Zone. In the video, Brolsma lip-synchs the song and dances while sitting at his desk in his bedroom. Yeah, that's it. Less than three months after the teen released the video filmed in his bedroom, it reached over a million views. Based on page impression figures collated by viral marketing company the Viral Factory, "Numa Numa Dance" was the second-most watched viral video of all time, with 700 million views, losing out only to "Star Wars Kid," made by Ghyslain Raza. Brolsma received mainstream media coverage from ABC's *Good Morning America*, NBC's *The Tonight Show* with Jay Leno, and VH1's *Best Week Ever*. He was voted the number one internet icon by *40 Greatest Internet Superstars* on VH1, beating the Star Wars Kid at number two. If you haven't seen the video, just google "numa numa guy."

Why all the hype? The historic significance of this silly video was that for the first time in history, a generation learned that anyone could reach the world from a computer in their bedroom. Generations born into the age of the internet are now forever connected to a global network and unlimited interaction through tiny cameras and microphones on smartphones, computers, and gaming consoles. The worldwide range of impact on every country's culture, methods of communication, and even the ability of new generations to converse interactively is still under evaluation. At least one thing is certain, though: All three have been changed forever.

The secret to online sales is understanding how the mind interprets information. When you look at an image or video online, the human brain will recognize and process images of human beings more quickly than objects. Even though you know that you are merely looking at a video image of a person on a computer screen or smartphone, your physiological system reacts just as if you are witnessing the events in real time. You have chemical and physiological reactions to images on computer screens, on billboards, and in print ads. Your conscious mind knows you are looking at a computer screen, but the human mind and body physiologically react to the image or movement of another human being, whether real or not.

What's even more powerful is that your mind learns faster from video images than from real human interactions. This is why Gen Y and Z children are glued to screens, watching other kids play with toys online and learning how to make "slime," and don't watch much network television. In less than fifteen years since its advent, digital technology has become so powerful, and the channels are so trusted, that on *Forbes'* 2018 World's Most Valuable Brands list, the top five are computer or online companies: Apple, Google, Microsoft, Facebook, and Amazon respectively.

If your business relies on computer and internet technologies for sales, keep in mind that every customer has a physiological reaction to every image and movement you communicate. In order for you to make decisions about what images and messages you communicate online, let's look at how people acquire and retain a yes.

THE THREE E'S OF YES

There are three components to making messages "stick" and getting people to do what you want them to do, especially online. This is not mind control. Messages stick when you listen deeply to customers, create an archetypal message architecture, and artfully craft mantras and visual hammers. To deliver your message, learn to pay attention to the three E's:

1) **Excite.** Excitement raises adrenalinee, the most powerful brain chemical when it comes to memory. To sell products and services online, you need to raise customer adrenaline levels. Increased adrenaline immediately dilates the pupils of the eye to let in more light, and it increases oxygen flow. Excitement, although temporary, causes people to make a decision, even a bad decision. Your organization's words, images, and videos need to evoke excitement if you want to sell. This alone is not enough, however.

2) **Educate.** When adrenaline is elevated, the brain is like flypaper for information. The excitement that raises adrenaline is designed for fight-or-flight. We then retain this reaction in great detail for the next fight-or-flight episode. In business you have to educate the customer at the intersection of excitement and the central idea you wish to get across. This is critical if you are to achieve your informational objective. Consumer product companies argue about the effectiveness of provocative images in advertising. Do they work? Yes. The problem is connecting an *evocative* image or video to the *educational* objective, and also getting the timing right. In addition—and this is very important— you need to do this with as few words as possible.

3) **Establish.** This is the component everyone forgets. Once you have raised adrenaline and educated at the highest saturation point of memory, you have to establish a behavior that reinforces

the contents of the message, image, or product you are looking to sell. Excitement and education are far less effective if you do not establish behavior. This is why so many transactional (e-commerce) websites have progress bars; they establish the behavior necessary to complete a transaction. Following any online transaction, you'll then need orchestrated follow-up emails, text messages, and notifications that establish positive behavior.

HOW AN AUCTIONEER USES THE THREE Es

My wife and I are on a nonprofit board of directors. We attend a number of fundraisers every year, and we see a lot of live auctions, silent auctions, and other creative ways to raise money and awareness for causes. Here's a simple example of the three E's used by an auctioneer.

The auctioneer holds up a hundred-dollar bill and announces that he is auctioning off the bill. This raises *excitement*; everyone thinks, *Could I bid and win one hundred dollars for less than one hundred dollars?* The auctioneer then quickly *educates* the attendees by saying, "I am starting the bidding at one dollar for this fresh hundred-dollar bill." This educates everyone about what the rules are—and the fact that they could pay less than one hundred dollars for the hundred-dollar bill gives all of them the confidence to raise their hand or paddle and bid.

The auctioneer then starts the bidding. Excitement grows, causing more irrational decisions. People generously raise their hands and the bidding goes up. Ultimately, the hundred-dollar bill is auctioned off for more than a hundred dollars. More important, the auctioneer has *established* audience behavior with the safety and confidence of a hand-raising bid, the excitement at the prospect of winning, and simulating the auction process. The first time I saw an auctioneer do this, the effect on the brain was obvious. The auctioneer uses the three E's to open the minds of the crowd to the concept of paying more than a hundred dollars for a hundred-dollar bill. It is the simplest form of profit: Get someone to pay more for something than its actual value.

HENRY IV AND THE POWER OF SOCIAL MEDIA

While we are still on the topic of selling things online, let's talk about the anatomy of yes in social media. Almost two decades after the internet arrived, most companies are still confused about how best to utilize social media. They are afraid of saying something wrong or not sharing the "voice of the brand." Some handle social media communications in-house, while others hire a social media agency or PR firm. Whether it's handled in-house or through an agency, massive mistakes have been made when companies try to tell their story on social media. McDonald's decided to have Ronald McDonald himself tweet under the #RonaldMcDonald hashtag—well, that invited a social media firestorm with thousands of people on Twitter who relentlessly bashed the brand.

Then the other quandaries: Do you restrict negative comments? (The brand Smucker's created a sticky mess for themselves doing this.) Should you go public with apologies? (By the way, the answer is always yes.) There are countless more stories of social media blunders that damaged brand reputations and cost companies millions.

Companies, products, and brands are continually on their own quest for identity, and they are not even aware of it. This is why many struggle with social media.

All you really need to know about the power and strategy of social media is spoken by Prince Harry in act 1, scene 2 of Shakespeare's *Henry IV*. First, though, a bit of background on Prince Harry: He doesn't like spending time in the castle with his father, King Henry IV. Instead, he goes to the local drinking establishment and matches wits and swordplay with his commoner friends, including a boisterous character named Falstaff. Prince Henry then conspires with his saloon friends, the commoners, to commit a crime. Henry (nicknamed Prince Hal) is left alone in the saloon in act 1 announcing his underlying plan, and his rationalized deception, in a soliloquy.

I've presented on each line of the soliloquy and its precise relevance to business strategy—but the golden nugget is *why* Prince Harry leaves the castle: to know, befriend, and even partner in crime with the common people, the people he is destined to rule. He not only engages with them; he listens to and understands them. Prince Harry, historically, becomes one of the greatest kings of England, Henry V, because he intimately knows and understands the people.

In the fundamentals of communication, social media is nothing new, yet it is the most effective sales tool in history, because it can deeply listen in scale.

WHY GETTING A YES ONLINE MATTERS

Getting a yes online matters if your business uses the internet as a transaction channel. It can be summed up this way:

· Listen deeply to your customers on social media channels. (This is the real purpose of social media.)

· Learn who your customers want to be (who the product will help them become) and why they need your product or service (sharper swords to defeat dragons).
· Swiftly deliver these powerful resources through interaction and simulation.

Recall the aforementioned research from the NTL Institute for Applied Behavioral Science: High school students in the United States retain only 5 percent of the information they read in class, 10 percent through lectures, and 75 percent through interaction and simulation. This can also be applied to sales—the vast majority responds to interaction and simulation. If you are selling something online, especially consumer products, always show a simulated product experience that the customer can play out in the reality of their own life. Your product stories need to be composed of elevated moments that incite your customers to follow. Just like Evel Knievel, Gary Brolsma, and even backyard daredevils in YouTube videos, you want to captivate your audience.

We're off to the thrift shop next. Unfortunately, you will learn that your charitable yes to donate clothing has little to do with charitable intent.

YOUR QUEST FOR YES
1. Does your website simulate the customer as a hero?
2. Who is the voice of your organization's social media?
3. Does your website have a call to action or a call to adventure?

17

Why You Really Donate Clothing

↓

We have been learning how people get what they want, and how businesses, brands, and people get others to say yes. It requires a combination of stories, values, and desires, looking the part, and deeply listening to the customer's fears and anxieties. Those fears can begin to surface during a transaction. Once you understand what's causing a customer's anxiety, you'll be in a position to deliver enlightenment. At Goodwill Industries we mapped the donation of clothing to better understand customer intent, and what we found was the opposite of conventional thought. It also gave us a strategy to inspire clothing donors to shop the stores of Goodwill.

Donating clothing might seem mundane and inconsequential, but choosing what to give away actually involves a neurological high-wire act within a detailed decision tree in order to reach a yes or a no. Let's examine how this works.

At one point during my time at Goodwill Industries, we had a clothing donation drought, which wasn't uncommon. The last thing I wanted to do was get reactive and stray from our existing annual plan. So we did what it takes to succeed: We became obsessed with winning, and kept digging for answers. The answer came late one night while reading a study published in the *Clothing and Textiles Research Journal.*[8]

Contrary to what we expected, I learned that clothing and furniture donors do not just donate in December each year for their tax deduction. They donate three to five times a year. The study showed that the key driver of the clothing and furniture donor is not charity—it's the completion of a consumption cycle.

We can use your closet as an example. You open your closet and notice how unorganized and cluttered it appears. You've got to get rid of some of this stuff. Cleaning your closet is the primary motivator for donating clothing. This first-level decision is an objective one, but it also causes the first level of anxiety: Are the clothes you want to donate in good shape or bad shape? This is not high anxiety; it's more in the neighborhood of half the anxiety you feel when you get a speeding ticket.

Some clothes in your closet have been there for more than ten years. Clothing is quite personal; it's very much connected with the Quest for Identity archetype. When I give talks on this subject, people have shared with me that they have held on to clothes from forty years ago. One gentleman confessed that he still had his black biker jacket, although he had not worn it in years and no longer owned a motorcycle. An Englishwoman couldn't part with an authentic kimono, even though she had only worn it once, more than twenty years ago.

In our quest for identity, as children most of us loved taking on characters and wearing costumes—and not only on Halloween.

---

[8] Jung E. Ha-Brookshire and Nancy N. Hodges, "Socially Responsible Consumer Behavior? Exploring Used Clothing Donation Behavior," *Clothing and Textiles Research Journal* 6 27, no. 3 (2009): 179–96, http://journals.sagepub.com/doi/abs/10.1177/0887302X08327199.

As adults, is it possible that we all hold on to "costumes" such as biker jackets and kimonos in an effort to stay connected to our childhood identities? What are the chances of that gentleman once again riding a motorcycle and wearing his jacket, or that woman adorning herself with a kimono and attending a tea ceremony?

Think about the articles of clothing you have kept the longest. They likely represent a tangible remnant of your life story that you want to revisit before you die. In studies conducted with people eighty years of age and older, researchers discovered that their greatest fear is not of death. In fact, it ranked as low as fourth. The top-ranked fear? Not to have sung their song; that is, not to have told their story—to have lived and died and have no one care. The clothing donor making a decision whether to discard a tangible item is really saying, "Do I want to leave this part of my story behind?"

If there is no associated story or identity attached to an article of clothing and the clothing is in bad shape, there is little guilt and the clothing is easily discarded—yes, thrown in the trash. It is a common misconception that Goodwill does not want your tattered clothing; even tattered clothing can be repurposed as rags used in machine shops or sold wholesale by weight.

If the clothes are in good shape, the anxiety level increases. The divide is now between high identity-based value and low identity-based value. How often have you held up a shirt or a pair of pants and said, "Did I really think this was a good look when I bought it?" Such an item has a low identity-based value.

Or you might say, "I was this person once, but I no longer have an attachment to that person." Again, the item has a low identity-based value. You feel a weak sense of guilt; these are clothes you will donate, but not discard. You will donate them because (a) you want to clean your closet, and (b) you deem them worthy of value based on your intent when you bought them.

The level at which you donate high identity-based clothing directly correlates with the amount of anxiety that is released. When the anxiety is released, the mind is now open to a new round of consumption. How much you empty your closet is directly related to how much you will replenish it.

At Goodwill, once we understood the motivation behind many of the donations we received, we shaped our business strategy to focus on what we labeled the "donor-not-yet-shopper." Goodwill had many suburban and high-net-worth clothing and furniture donors, but these donors would never set foot in our thrift stores. We saw this as both a problem and a huge opportunity—they were donating goods about fifty yards away from the store entrance.

The first experiment to get high-net-worth donors to shop Goodwill stores was at the Goodwill in San Francisco. Goodwill San Francisco opened a boutique thrift shop in Marin, California, dubbed Georgi & Willow. I went to visit the store and the folks in San Francisco, and within a year we opened a higher-end boutique in Southern California. It was a sucess. The average shopping cart sale at Goodwill's thrift stores was around fourteen dollars, while the average boutique sale was around twenty-four dollars. We also built an affinity on social media with the donor-not-yet-shopper.

The anatomy of yes in clothing donation and sales came from realizing that charitable intent is not the primary motivator among donors. The bigger opportunity we seized was intersecting with this consumption cycle and then hiring people who had overcome physical and cognitive barriers in life to work at Goodwill. Shopping aside, the greatest stories at Goodwill I discovered were about the courageous parents of children with physical and cognitive disabilities. So many of the parents I met and interviewed said that Goodwill was the place to go when there was no other place to go.

YOUR QUEST FOR YES

1. How are your company's products or services part of a consumption cycle?
2. What is the oldest and most prized garment in your closet?

Act III

A Call to
Adventure

18

Hunters and Farmers

↓

Thought leaders and TED talks often focus on how to achieve goals and fulfill your desires. What I seldom hear from those, though, is how to achieve goals, get what you want—*and raise children*. How to be both a "hunter" and a "farmer." My wife and I have three children, and in their early years, I lost time with them. My year at Disney Store took me out of the house at 7:00 a.m. and back home after 9:00 p.m., five days a week; I often didn't see them until the weekend. Is it important to spend time with your children? Yes. Is it important to wholeheartedly commit yourself to your work, because that enables you to afford to have a family and provide for them? Absolutely. Some call this the "work-life balance"—another way of saying "pain-pleasure balance."

You can think of yourself as having dual roles: You are both a hunter and a farmer. Which one are you today? When you are hunting, you are selling, engineering, creating, and dragon slaying. When you are farming, you are cultivating relationships, increasing your wealth, and growing your family. Instead of thinking about it as a work-life balance, think of it as a hunter-farmer balance. Give purpose to those activities that will feed your family *and* your soul.

HUNTING, FARMING, AND PLAYING BALL IN THE HOUSE

Years ago, my oldest daughter started playing youth soccer. She liked to practice by kicking a soccer ball in the house. This was not good—things got broken. I called my brother John, a two-time national NSCAA Soccer Coach of the Year. I asked him what I should buy to help her train for soccer. He told me there wasn't anything I could buy, that all the existing training products were basically junk. He also told me that the secret to soccer training is using both feet equally, or what's called bilateral training. He said that if a player can juggle a soccer ball 175 times from foot to foot, they will become a great player.

That seemed simple enough. Then I asked him, "If you could have any training product in the world, something that doesn't yet exist, what would it be?" He said it would be an antigravity ball—one that would move in slow motion. That was the spark. Using a balloon and some painter's tape, I tried to simulate an antigravity ball, something that would spin and react like a real soccer ball but move in slow motion. And something that didn't break things in the house!

It didn't work well—it was lopsided because of the knot in the balloon—but I knew I was on to something. Over the next few months, I continued experimenting with other materials such as bladders (the rubber bag inside a football) and weights, and together as a family, we eventually built a ball that had never been built before.

All three of my kids continued using the ball—designing it, refining it, coloring on it, and having a lot of fun in the process. My wife sewed the outer shell designs on our kitchen table, and we came up with more than fifty iterations. It had now become an obsession. With much research and despite a lot of frustration, many late nights, and multiple trips to sewing factories, what had started as a balloon with painter's tape was now a patentable product. We also started spending real money on it. While farming with my family in making a ball they could train and play with in the house, we started hunting a market opportunity to manufacture and sell a new product.

Fast-forward to 2016. With a series of patent and trademark applications, videos, and testing, we signed a cooperative development and manufacturing deal with the largest US ball maker. We named the sports training ball the VICTURY ball. It allows any athlete to "Train Without Limits." We also invented a play ball called the OllyBall that allows any kid to "Play Without Limits." Both of these products came about because of a crisis of things breaking and two parents repeatedly yelling, "Don't play ball in the house!"

As a family, we spent several joyful years engineering an impact-absorption ball that can be hit very hard without breaking things. I've been asked how many hours I put into the product. I really have no idea. Someone asked me, "What if it fails?" The answer was easy. The product already had succeeded. The ball had brought so much joy to our family over the years, it couldn't fail. Our goal now was to bring that same joy to parents, kids, and athletes.

We took another risk and showed the ball at the International Toy Fair in New York City. The impossible goal was to have a major retailer include our ball in their fall 2018 line and place it in all US stores. We knew that if the product was not received well, it would be dead before it ever made it to market.

What happened next was beyond anything we had imagined. Major retailers who stopped by the demonstration booth at the

International Toy Fair could not stop playing with the ball. Out of 150,000 toys, we were recognized as one of the "12 Best Toys from the 2018 International Toy Fair" by *Fatherly* magazine. At the final editing of this book, the product was picked up by a major retailer. And then, we become a finalist for Toy of the Year at the "Oscars of the Toy Industry." The verdict is still out at the publishing of this book.

The entire experience taught me lessons from every dimension of business—from concept and failed prototypes to invention, presentation, forecasting, and sales. Within your company—and within your friends and family—you, too, can find this same joy and discover a way for others to share your joy. This was truly an experience of spending days and nights as a hunter building a brand, and as a farmer with my family.

YOUR QUEST FOR YES

1. When are you a farmer?
2. When are you a hunter?
3. How do you achieve balance between the two?

19

Why Your Organization Exists

↓

There is a chronology of the five archetypes in the anatomy of yes. Your organization has been walking through this chronology since its foundation and the formation of the entity. It is why your organization exists.

THE ORGANIZATIONAL JOURNEY

When your organization began, there was an instinctual **quest for identity**. You began defining the company and what it stood for. The company started with transactions and became unique in the way it performed those transactions. This formed a corporate identity, which was represented by a name and some symbol or unique representation of the company name. At this moment you became a living organization and began building your reputation. This was your brand's equity.

The organization continued to "tune the instrument" that triggered the most attention and sales. As it did, your company moved into a heroic role in delivering its products or services.

Next, your organization was met with fierce tests, competitive enemies, and some good partners and allies. You hired more warriors to fight **dragons** and capture **treasures**. This was, and is, the story of survival.

As your organization matured and became deft in battle, there occurred one or more **descents into the underworld**. This is where the organization was hit with a financial downturn, lawsuit, or bankruptcy protection, and looked straight into the face of an abyss. When the reorganization, buyout, merger, reconciliation, or settlement was resolved, your organization, led by its people, emerged stronger.

As the organization continued to overcome barriers and grow, you and your colleagues found yourselves repeatedly solving and fixing problems. This repeated pattern of talent and service allowed the organization to restore itself from the descent into the under-world, and it helped customers and fellow employees in their own **restoration of the wasteland**.

Finally, your organization will continue its **quest for the holy grail**, its eternal life. The life span of companies in the S&P 500 index has decreased from sixty-one years in 1958 to just eighteen years, measured at the end of 2015. The only way eternal life is achieved within an organization is through the success and actualization of its people's dreams. Your organization is a living, breathing entity; it is larger than the sum of its people. It exists to create a profound effect on the people who join the company as they begin to slay their own dragons, achieve their own treasures, and seek their own holy grails.

As you personally grow in your career and slay dragons, pay close attention to your weapons and shields. The most powerful weapon you will own is wisdom through knowledge, and the strongest shield will be your mental resolve through adversity and your faith in finding things unseen.

A CALL TO ADVENTURE

In business, your customers are heroes on a quest for something. You, personally and professionally, are also a living character within a storyline. You are embroiled right now in defeating dragons, emerging from an abyss, restoring wastelands, or on your final quest for the holy grail. If you truly want to accomplish or overcome something, I have a methodology for you to achieve your goals.

First, think about a high-stakes goal you have that is likely to fail. You will have a far greater chance of getting what you want by using this method, but it requires that you follow a couple of rules. If you have a powerful goal in mind, now is the time to handcuff yourself to achieving it. Here's how:

> On a blank piece of paper, write these words:
> "I, [your name], am willing to make the necessary sacrifices to [your goal], because it will [why you want it] and [why you need it]."

At our home, my wife and I bolted a solid, one-inch-thick block of walnut onto our kitchen wall. On that block each member of our family handwrote a public testimony and literally nailed it to the block of wood for all of us to see every morning. Each of my daughters made aggressive goals, and they achieved them in less than six months. My public testimony in 2016 said this:

> "I, Joseph Burke, am willing to make the necessary sacrifices to launch a new product, write a book, produce a film, and serve

my clients and family. This work will feed my family. This work will feed my soul."

Take the piece of paper and place it on your kitchen wall, in your office, or somewhere else you routinely look at throughout the day. Then, take a picture of it and post it at anatomyofyes.com/story and we will share it with our community of enablers to help hold all of us accountable to our goals. The power of this public testimony will handcuff you to the hard work at hand. Your family, circle of friends, and work colleagues will hold you accountable to your commitments. As you contemplate what necessary sacrifices you are willing to make, ask yourself if it will likely fail. If it will likely fail, do it. That is the true definition of courage.

If you have answered all the questions in the "Your Quest for Yes" sections, you have learned that trying to *get* a customer to say yes is very different from *empowering* a customer on their quest for yes. Stories structured in archetypes are the most effective way to sell anything. From the power of the parent-child relationship displayed in Disney movies to battling the dragons of competition to restoring the wastelands that exist in your customers' lives, the anatomy of yes is why your organization exists.

In advertising we often hear the phrase "call to action." The root of archetypal patterns, and the hero's quest, are stitched into this single phrase. The best call to action is a *call to adventure* that propels the protagonist in search of identity, treasure, a descent, a restoration, or a legacy. Be sure that your organization's call to action is a true call to adventure—one that catapults your customers on their journey through the five archetypes in the anatomy of yes.

The questions throughout this book were created for you to find your organization's story behind every sale. If you gather with the leaders in your company once a week and share your individual answers to these questions, you will find your true story behind every sale.

YOUR QUEST FOR YES

1. What goal is your organization willing to make the necessary sacrifices for?
2. How can you better empower your clients or customers to reach a yes?

EPILOGUE

↓

This book was written in forty-six hours on a train in 2016. Today, May 20, 2018, I finish the final edits with the team at Wellspring. A few months back, a young man asked to meet with me because he wanted to write a book. With a suggested sequence of steps, today that young man boarded a train in Chicago and set out for San Francisco to write his own book over a fifty-three-hour ride. He began his own hero's adventure today. If I was able to play a role, it was to be a "sword maker" and equip him with the tools to build his book. As for me, my wife and I are planning another train ride—this time through Europe—to write *The Story of Yes*. It will be a book about why we exist.

ABOUT THE AUTHOR

↓

Joseph G. Burke has spoken on archetypal patterns in business strategy as a presenter and panelist in more than one hundred public forums, including Boeing, USC Marshall School of Business, and the NGCX summit.

Burke is a Hylan Academic Scholarship recipient, former NCAA athlete, and a graduate of Rochester Institute of Technology. He created a start-up digital agency at the age of twenty-one, served as the national brand director of Disney Store and teen retailer Wet Seal, and was VP of marketing for Goodwill Industries, and appeared as an actor in more than twenty-five film and TV roles, Burke currently owns a creative advertising agency and a toy company, and collaborates on a portfolio of projects, including producing films and developing screenplays. His proudest achievement is tempering dual roles as hunter and farmer with his wife, Ellen, a university instructor, and their three children.